Active Learning in a Family Day Care Setting

Susan McCartney

Illustrated by Fran Schultz Greenhaus

 GoodYearBooks

An Imprint of ScottForesman
A Division of HarperCollinsPublishers

Dedication

I would like to dedicate this book to my children—Joseph, Kate, and Hannah.

Joseph—for allowing me to see two sides of work;

Kate—for helping me determine which side to work on; and

Hannah—for allowing me to do the work.

GoodYearBooks

are available for most basic curriculum subjects plus many enrichment areas. For more GoodYearBooks, contact your local bookseller or educational dealer. For a complete catalog with information about other GoodYearBooks, please write:

GoodYearBooks
ScottForesman
1900 East Lake Avenue
Glenview, IL 60025

Preface

I wanted to explore child development to increase my confidence and competence in meeting the growing needs and learning capabilities of my own children and the children in my care.

Much of the child development resource material currently available is written in a textbook style that is not appropriate for the daily ongoing routine of caring for young children. Many of these books just present the philosophies and theories of developmentalists and early childhood research studies.

Understanding the various cognitive and physical levels of a child's development increases one's ability to provide an atmosphere that benefits the total development of each child. Once an understanding of child development is realized, trust, respect, and encouragement must be gathered to champion the child's personal and social growth. A home care provider needs to know how to apply these philosophies and theories in direct, practical terms.

My goal then is to provide balanced experiences that will match the intellectual and physical abilities of each child. If we learn more about child development we can put to use what we know is needed: an amicable atmosphere with stimulating language experiences and developmentally appropriate activities that help children develop visual skills, verbal skills, and creative thoughts.

I emphasize the importance of meeting a child's holistic needs through affective/emotional activities and cognitively oriented thinking. As caregivers, we need to enhance a child's perception and social experiences and affirm a child's self-esteem, sense of belonging, and confidence to use his or her own mind. The quest is now to become more of what we already are and to help children be all that they can imagine.

Acknowledgments

I would like to thank Dr. June Moss Handler for giving me the encouragement and raw guidance I needed to "see" myself; and for her gentle faith and wisdom that I have come to trust.

I would like to thank my husband for being my personal thesaurus and for providing both the mental and physical work space I needed to do my work.

Contents

■
■
■

PART ONE

The Need to Understand Child Development

Chapter 1

The Cognitive and Physical Growth of Newborns

■

Early Infant Responses

Do you view the newborn as a helpless, dependent creature incapable of anything except crying, feeding, burping, spitting up, sleeping, and needing a diaper change? This view, though seemingly factual for some days, is incomplete because it overlooks a great deal of competent behavior newborns are capable of performing. A newborn can see, hear, touch, smell, and feel pain. The nervous system is not fully developed at birth, but is capable of receiving stimulation—though stimulation should not be in excess because an infant's responses are at this moment limited.

■

Vision

Of all of the five senses, vision is the most important. The eye, while not fully developed at birth, can see light and dark and some degree of color. Did you know that a newborn can fixate on a light and within just a few days can follow or track a moving light or shiny object? For example, if we move our heads slowly to one side or hold a finger in front of the baby and move it slowly to see if the baby follows, they do!

I can recall a moment in the hospital the day after my daughter was born. A well-wishing visitor had tied a colorful helium balloon onto my bed. When the nurse brought Kate in for her feeding, Kate caught sight of the balloon's ribbon and followed the ribbon right up to the shiny balloon. She was less than twenty-four hours old!

Over the next two months an infant's focal distances rapidly increase. Did you know that by the fourth month an infant can focus as well as an adult? What is most interesting to me in providing direct personal child care is knowing how selective and attentive an infant can be in responding to certain stimuli.

❏ **IF** infants prefer complex patterns, as opposed to colors, such as a human face, a bull's-eye design, light/dark images, and shiny objects;

❏ **THEN** we can design our own patterns now knowing what interests babies most.

❏ **HOW?** Draw your own design of a face or target with a black marker on a white paper plate or on the inside of a cardboard gift box. Prop it up next to the baby or hang as a mobile that faces the infant.

Lie your baby near a window. The light filtering in attracts their attention and the window panes and curtains offer contrasts of light and dark stimulation.

❏ **WHY?** The areas of contrast on a face and the light/dark patterns stimulate nerve cells and coordination between the infant's two eyes. The results of infant vision experiments show that faces and light/dark contrasts are focal points infants attend to longest. Let the results of such studies guide your own simple creations of visual stimulation. When purchasing crib or stroller mobiles use the results of these studies to buy what will interest infants most.

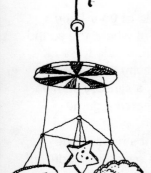

■

Hearing

There is substantial sound discrimination shortly after birth. If you are caring for infants, you can see the baby react with a startle response and show an increased alertness to high frequency sounds.

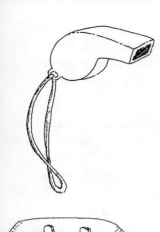

❏ **IF** a high frequency sound such as a child's scream, a shrill sound of a whistle, or the ring of a telephone stimulates the sense of hearing;

❏ **THEN** you can increase the infant's awareness of sounds within their environment.

❏ **HOW?** Respond verbally to all of the vocalization attempts baby produces.

Describe the sounds babies hear to reassure them: "Let's go answer the telephone." "Did you hear that loud whistle?" Your voice is comforting. Though the baby doesn't understand your words your voice soothes and distracts from any excessive stimulation the infant may not be able to handle.

Conduct your own simple listening experiments:

• Snap your fingers.

• Whisper.

• Make clicking noises on one side of your baby's head until the baby turns to look at where the sound is coming from. Repeat on the other side to see if baby follows the sound. If this activity is repeated often enough, then besides being a sensory stimulation for hearing, you have just created a game adding the element of anticipation. With your repeated actions the baby will turn it's head in the direction of the sound *before* the sound is produced!

❏ **WHY?** You want children to respond to sound and to be able to tolerate some degree of noise. Providing different types of stimulation helps you determine the baby's threshold for noise. When you learn the rhythm and sensitivity threshold of an infant in your care, your responses will help produce a pleasurable, harmonious, and trusting relationship.

Oftentimes infants become overly stimulated by noises in their environment and may need soothing.

❏ **IF** you need to soothe an infant, the low pitch of continuous sounds produces **habituation**—a term used when the movements of an infant's body remain calm and at ease. Breathing slows, legs stop kicking, arms rest—the body's movements remain quiet and peaceful.

❏ **THEN** by soothing an infant you are teaching a child to feel secure within that environment. You are helping a child gain your trust and the need to be comforted will be met.

❏ **HOW?** Lullabies, gentle classical music, rocking, humming, "soft conversation," and even the sound of children playing quietly nearby are examples of listening techniques that can soothe an infant without producing excessive responses.

❏ **WHY?** Infants learn very early to expect a response from their caregivers caused by their own actions. Our response demonstrates to infants they have power—the power to make us respond. You learn the infant's behavior and temperament and respond accordingly. This harmonious, continuous interaction builds reliance; and at the same time autonomy—that quality of reacting and developing on our own.

When appropriate responses are received you feel good about yourself. You feel you did the right thing for the benefit of the child. This positive feeling supports a mutual, loving, friendly, tender relationship with the infant. When infants receive our appropriate encouraging responses they learn to feel reliance. This trusting foundation greatly assists the character of the infant and the confidence in yourself.

■

Taste

❏ **IF** studies have shown that infants will make sucking responses when given milk, glucose, and sterile water but will cease this gratified sucking behavior and grimace when presented with a salty, bitter, or acidic solution;

❏ **THEN** I do not encourage taste tests with infants in my child-care program. I have heard many parents, complain about mothers, fathers, in-laws, and grandparents giving babies "just a little taste" of ice cream, whipped cream, granulated sugar, salty pretzels, or frozen pudding pops.

❏ **HOW?** At our initial interview, I ask parents for information concerning their child's likes/dislikes, allergic reactions and/or food intolerances. With infants, I suggest that parents bring their own prepared formula and bottles, expressed breast milk and/or jars of baby food and cereals.

❏ **WHY?** I believe parents can do their own taste testing experiments with their babies and furnish me with the results for additions or substitutions to their child's menu. With this age parents can enjoy their own experiments.

■

Empathy For All Ages

Personalities and behaviors are different with each and every child. Each child is born with a certain individuality. These differences influence the way we respond and react to each child. Through our interactions with children we uncover certain sensitivities—feelings and particular ways children show their emotions.

❏ **IF** you observe a child in your care with the capacity to feel empathy—that quality of being able to relate to another person's feelings;

❏ **THEN** encourage this quality.

❏ **HOW?** I have witnessed the facial expressions of a six month old change from pleasantly content to a grimace of obvious distress upon hearing the crying of a three year old. As I carried the baby nearer to the crying boy she smiled, cooed, and laughed trying to elicit the same response from him. I experimented by moving the infant away from him and she fussed and squirmed until she saw him again. She repeated her pleasantries for him. And he was consoled.

I have observed a two year old pat and rub the back of a toddler who performed a clumsy somersault. You have to recognize such sensitivity and tell empathic children how sweet and wonderful they are for trying to comfort or console another person.

I have seen preschoolers offer an infant toys to play with when the infant begins to fuss. I have to respond by affirming their good-hearted actions and thoughtfulness.

I have had a three year old hand me a new diaper when an infant began to fuss—an understanding that the infant's fretful signal may warrant a diaper change. I thanked the three year old for her attentiveness and told her how much I appreciated the way she helped me take care of the baby.

❏ **WHY?** At any age, with all positive behavior and cooperative participation, children *need* to know they are doing the right thing. They need you to tell them. They want to please. Whether it is showing early signs of empathy or meeting your expectations, childrens' responses and actions have to be recognized by the adults in their lives. We have to learn to offer a child a positive affirmation that acknowledges their actions and offers our approval. Children seek our approval. When their conduct warrants our approval they deserve to receive it. One of our primary concerns as parents and child-care workers is to facilitate a child's learning about how to relate and interact with another person's feelings. Empathy is a profound trait that we should recognize verbally. That way we help children learn to share an emotional and intellectual accord with others.

Chapter 2

How Do Children Learn to Think and Act?

■

The Development of Grasping and Reaching Skills

Babies use their senses to develop a growing awareness of the many sights and sounds of the people and objects in their environment. Now with the physical development of reaching out, grabbing, and holding onto people and things in their environment, they are ready and eager to apply their senses.

Month by month each new physical development leads naturally to increased intellectual development. The more children know about their bodies the more their minds can absorb.

The body and the mind of a young child operate in unison. The physical development of reaching stimulates the learning process of putting toys and objects right into the mouth. Children learn concepts such as hard/soft, loud/quiet, and warm/cold by exploring and sampling their fingers, toes, toys, and loved ones with their senses. The body:mind is this combined effort of physical development and intellectual development. Discovery through sensory stimulation develops the body:mind.

Grasping skills (prehension) are shown to occur in sequential stages. The appropriate stimulation that meets the infant's skill during each stage governs and encourages the baby's acquisition of grasping techniques. Detailed studies by B. White (1967, 1971) have suggested that stimulation must be appropriate to both the age of the baby and the abilities of the baby because too much stimulation may be irritating and/or confusing to an infant and may fail to develop the baby's interest and development of motor skills. These sequential stages are presented here for parents and child-care workers to enrich the environment for infants.

❑ **IF** at Stage 1 (1–2 months) there are impulsive movements;

❑ **THEN** these movements are pure reflexes, not a conscious effort to grasp. Though a newborn can grasp a finger and hold it securely, the appropriate stimulation at this early stage is to hold the newborn and feed the baby when hungry. Through the holding and feeding times all of the baby's senses are aroused by you: the smelling and tasting, your "soft conversation," the intent stare of the baby, and your gentle touch.

❑ **IF** at Stage 2 (2–3 months) there is a random chance at grasping;

❑ **THEN** the baby's hands are still moving randomly with no hand-eye coordination. It is still too soon for babies to have rattles and toys because with this random motion of arms flailing and swinging they usually end up batting themselves in the head. Babies are more concerned with the looking, feeling, hearing, smelling, and tasting interactions provided by parents or child care-giver. Babies process this sensory stimulation into vital information.

❑ **IF** at Stage 3 (3–4 months) objects grasped now can reach the mouth;

❑ **THEN** the baby has developed the coordination between their hand movements and sucking. There are very sensitive nerve endings on the infant's lips. The stimulation received by touching fingers and objects to the mouth increases sensory learning. The hands are still moving in and out of baby's line of vision, however they can always reach the mouth. Now is the time to start dangling toys and objects from string or yarn onto anything in close proximity to the infant.

❑ **HOW?** If your baby is lying on the floor or sitting in an infant seat, place a chair in front of the baby

with rattles, squeaky toys, or plush objects dangling from it. The chair should be close enough for baby to swing at, kick, grasp, and reach the objects even if it is by chance. Interchange the toys with safe common household items such as a wooden spoon, a washcloth, or shower curtain rings clipped together. Walk around your house and use your imagination to create your own stimulating sensory experiences for your baby or the babies in your care.

❑ **IF** at Stage 4 (4–5 months) hands and objects can be viewed simultaneously but still not intentionally;

❑ **THEN** the eyes can follow the hands but hand-eye coordination is not yet developed. Grasping babies propped into a sitting position gain an entirely new and different perspective on their environment. Studies by W. Dennis and Yvonne Sayegh (1965) compared infants that spent most of their first year lying on their backs only looking up at objects with infants given a chance to sit up, handle, and play with a variety of simple objects. Despite this seemingly small amount of stimulation, the babies' developmental age jumped dramatically just by being propped up.

❑ **IF** at Stage 5 (5–6 months) vision can directly lead to grasping;

❑ **THEN** the hand grasps what the eye observes as well as the eye following what the hand can grasp. Reaching out leads to turning over, creeping, then crawling. This whole new process adds new avenues of development and learning. The onset of moving about vastly increases the infant's perceptual, social, and emotional world as he/she expands their ability to initiate social contact while exploring their environment. The mastery of a skill such as crawling and walking as psychologist Erik Erikson (1963) points out, helps to make children part of their culture—the child acquires a status that contributes to their necessary and budding self-esteem. The child who begins to crawl, then walk, leaves behind their infant status.

The Importance of Conveying Trust

❑ **IF** a child is about to move into another room out of your sight;

❑ **THEN** you might say playfully, "Where are you going?" or "I can't find you."

❑ **WHY?** The sound of your voice is the security the child needs for reassurance. The child knows by your words that their moving away is recognized and acknowledged by you and meets with your approval. The child has gained your trust and is now free to think about this new independent venture of exploring on his or her own, comfortably knowing you know.

Children benefit from this atmosphere of being allowed to instinctually "feel" their surroundings. Remember they have been learning about their surroundings through the use of their senses: vision, touch, taste, hearing, and smelling. Now, combined with new motor skills they can organize into memory all of the sensory experiences they have absorbed and you have provided. During this sensorimotor stage children's thinking skills organize, sort out, and register connections that integrate and unite the people, the places, and the objects that they have come to know into meaningful representations.

The Greater Value of Trust: Exploratory Behavior

❑ **IF** learning to move about means leaving behind the status of babyhood;

❑ **THEN** children must be given plenty of opportunities to explore, to create, and to re-create their thoughts and emotions.

But that is only one facet of their learning. Children need our encouragement to explore touching, tast-

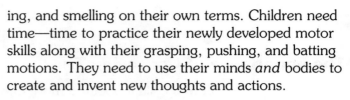

ing, and smelling on their own terms. Children need time—time to practice their newly developed motor skills along with their grasping, pushing, and batting motions. They need to use their minds *and* bodies to create and invent new thoughts and actions.

❑ **IF** we encourage children to think and feel and do on their own, with our approval;

❑ **THEN** a child's sense of self also develops. You can't separate them. A sense of self to a child means freedom to think and learn within a safe environment. The child finds increasing satisfaction in acting upon, exploring, and getting to know their social and physical world.

❑ **HOW?** Studies by Dr. M. Ainsworth (1978) proved that children showed distress at being left by their parents or other primary caregiver. However, they showed *no* distress when they left this attachment figure to explore.

❑ **WHY?** There are two motivational systems working simultaneously. One is called **detachment**—the motivated feeling of wanting to move away, gain independence, separate from you. However, to keep the mind and body in check as a self-regulatory process, detachment coexists with **attachment**—the need to be near familiar and loved faces. Both systems interact. A child detaches from their parents or primary caregiver during their second year motivated by the desire to be competent; to learn more about the world they live in. They learn to become thinkers and doers by touching, taking apart, putting together, and figuring out on their own. They learn how to *evoke* our responses through smiling. They learn how to get our attention. They will soon learn to say, "No!"

This striving to explore and try out new experiences—risk new feats—coexists with the desire to be close to familiar and loved people. Children that have learned to feel secure in their attachments feel safe to explore and develop their own sense of self. Detachment is not the opposite of attachment, nor

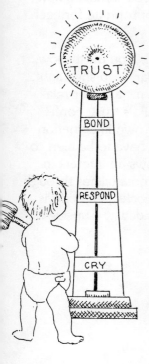

does it signal the end of attachment. From exploring on their own, children absorb new knowledge and learn new abilities both physically and intellectually.

Remember that your constant, reliable care promotes a child's sense of *trust*. This consistency in care enables children to learn to tolerate frustrations and to delay immediate gratification because they know you care and can be trusted to meet their needs.

❏ **IF** a child's needs are not consistently met, they can develop a sense of mistrust.

❏ **THEN** they learn to react to frustration with anxiety and whining; they may give up hope. Trust appears to underlie how a child will attack a problem be it simple or complex.

❏ **HOW?** If children feel trust they learn to believe they are in control of what they do and of what happens to them. Without a sense of trust children may feel that what they do makes little difference or impact on you or the world around them.

❏ **WHY?** Children need our guidance, our reassurance, and our approval to initially venture forth safely and independently.

■

Trust, Exploration, and Thinking

❏ **IF** you play with a toy or a game with a child;

❏ **THEN** you are sharing your time. This encourages children to think playfully, understand better and remember their own actions. This way they can reach out beyond what is and speculate on what might be. While playing and observing each child you learn and discover how each child thinks and what each one is capable of understanding.

❏ **HOW?** When you observe, listen, and play alongside, you automatically expand childrens' ideas and language. By listening to their ideas and language you learn the plateau of their development and seek ways to advance it. By offering suggestions and alternatives while they play, you stimulate new ideas that are developmentally appropriate for each level of understanding.

❏ **WHY?** You are the role model. You must show, educate, and explain the unfamiliar. You shed light. Sharing your time with a child forms a closer relationship which in turn builds a child's trust, confidence, and self-esteem. Use your own imagination to make the familiar strange! We have to be alert to the kinds of things each child shows an interest in and gravitates toward. Releasing possibilities through play, however strange or silly, unlocks perceptions that help children learn to think sideways, upside down, poetically, and in color.

Chapter 3

Innovative Ideas, Creative Thoughts, and Language Development

■

Which Comes First: Thinking or Language?

To feel secure enough to move about on one's own involves thinking on one's own. Exploring, imitating, playing, and remembering while moving about are the interrelated proceedings needed for cognitive growth. Through cognitive growth new tasks abound.

One of our top priorities as caregivers is to help children learn to think for themselves. This process starts even in infancy when we begin to ask very young children questions like:

"What do you see there?"

"Are you warm?"

"Are you hungry now?"

"Can I get you a blanket?"

"What would you like for lunch?"

Asking questions infers a pause—an allotted time to answer. This time gives us a chance to organize our own thoughts and immediate actions. Even though we know the children are too young to respond verbally to our questions, we can offer countless opportunities for them to listen to language and store answers provided by our actions. Questions seem to get and hold their attention. Take a moment to think of what happens if an infant just happens to gurgle or gesture at you after you speak. The vocal sounds and actions of a young child require you to react immediately. A verbal response or perhaps a smile, a hug, or even a look of concern encourages all attempts of communicating.

For a child to learn how to use words meaningfully thereafter, their first two years of life are basically intent on establishing active, secure relationships between their play, their actions, and their routines with the accompanying words of their caregivers. Language develops gradually through these very interactions. Swiss psychologist Jean Piaget's (1955) work of observing, interpreting, and analyzing child behavior and development proves these necessary interactions are precursors of language.

You can draw your own conclusions. When you interact with young children or when you observe them, you will discover that each of their thoughts could become a scene. Each scene, or combination of ideas, could then evolve into a meaningful mental event. Each idea holds meaning. These very ideas, thoughts, and actions are knowledge being registered and stored. Understanding the meaning of words and phrases is the fundamental knowledge that is subsequently released to target language, the ability to speak.

■

Aiming at the Right Side of the Brain

Child and language development theories are powerful tools that must be considered in order to design activities and experiences that are developmentally appropriate for young children in our care. While each theory provides its own determinant of language development, caregivers require a daily, ongoing application of these theories. Often, the well-meaning charts and graphs, always captioned "ages approximate," and used to summarize these theories, are intended to explain milestones of communication for us.

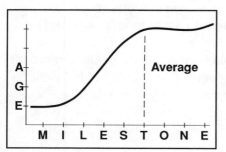

But they won't help if we think we have to rely and adhere to them. With patience, time, stimulating activities, and developmentally appropriate experiences, children will achieve each milestone. By reading various child development studies and by focusing on children acquiring thinking skills, recognizing their modes of expression, their peer relationships, and patterns of physical growth, you can observe, interact, and appreciate each one as a creatively clear thinker, good listener, problem solver, initiator, and/or imitator. Caregivers need to view children in this holistic, or "Big Picture" engagement.

❏ **IF** we were to concentrate on only one theory and only on one milestone chart;

❏ **THEN** we would ill serve our children.

❏ **HOW?** To see children holistically, in the "Big Picture" concept, we have to observe and seek meaning behind their thoughts (cognition), their feelings (emotionality), their play and language (socialization), and their physical abilities.

Clinical and experimental evidence shows the brain to be split into two cognitively functioning hemispheres. For us to view children fairly and holistically, we need to know what's happening in both sides of the brain. Each hemisphere processes information differently; unique to its hemispheric capacity. The hemispheres share information through a constant flow and exchange. From the research of Howard Gardner (1980) and Betty Edwards (1979), the methods of learning and processing this information and knowledge is handled differently by the brain depending upon how the information is presented to us and then how we perceive it.

❏ **WHY?** Perception and learning are dependent on which hemisphere gathers, assembles, and processes our ideas, words, and actions. One side may be dominant, able to assemble and process ideas, words, and actions into meaningful representation.

Can you decide how your brain is functioning? The following list looks at ways each side of the brain is processing information.

Left Brain Hemisphere	Right Brain Hemisphere
intellect	intuition
convergent	divergent
digital	analogic
secondary	primary
abstract	concrete
directed	free
propositional	imaginative
analytic	relational
lineal	nonlineal
rational	intuitive
sequential	multiple
analytic	holistic
objective	subjective
successive	simultaneous

Source: J. E. Bogen, "Some Educational Aspects of Hemisphere Specialization" from B. Edwards, *Drawing on the Right Side of the Brain* (Los Angeles: J. P. Tarcher, 1979). Used with permission.

❏ **IF** there are many combinations of right-left brain dominance, all of which are normal;

❏ **THEN** most children are not totally left-brained or totally right-brained.

❏ **HOW?** There are children who have a dominant right hemisphere with their behavior characteristics and language in the left hemisphere. On the other hand, there are children who have a dominant left hemisphere where behavior and language development emanates from the right. Some children show extreme dominances while others vary in the degree of dominance of either hemisphere. As caregivers we need to be able to identify a child's preference for thinking patterns. Daydreaming, talking in phrases, doodling, and making faces are considered right-brain functions. Each of these is a thought process in itself. Opportunities to use both verbal cues and visual images could stimulate and develop both sides of the brain. Right-brain thought processes working with left-brain characteristics help children learn to analyze their thoughts and actions and evaluate them.

There are three methods to help us determine a child's dominant hemisphere: observation; open-ended questioning which profiles the functioning of a left and/or right thinker and learner; and a dominance checklist.

Checklists from split-brain research have been derived from evidential studies on learning and memory brain functions. Checklisting the characteristics of each hemisphere helps us think of ways to help children exercise the special abilities stemming from both sides.

Left Hemisphere	Right Hemisphere
Verbal, speaking skills	Nonverbal, perceptive skills
Thinks through sequential, ordered data; routines	Understands complex relationships not necessarily logical
Critical thinking	Divergent thinking
Feelings of happiness	Sense of humor
Fine muscle control	Large muscle control, spatial relationships
Listening strengths	Visual strengths
Writing skills	Creative, insightful
Uses well-tested, step-by-step problem solving techniques	Sees the whole problem and takes problem solving steps

Parents and caregivers can better appreciate individual strengths and methods of learning.

Analytic learners are always seeking facts. They need to know what the experts think. Their learning comes by thinking through ideas to form reality. More interested in ideas and concepts than people, they would rather critique information and collect data. School settings seem to be designed specifically for these types of learners. Their favorite question would be *What?*

Common sense learners need to know how things work. They edit reality and seek usability. They learn by testing theories in ways that seem sensible. Common sense learners perceive information abstractly and process it actively by using hands-on experiences. Their strength comes from practical applications of ideas functioning through inferences drawn from sensory experiences. Their favorite question would be *How does it work?*

Dynamic learners seek hidden possibilities and excitement in order to find out what can be done with things. They lead by energizing people to learn by trial and error and self-discovery. They are adaptable to change and relish in it, excelling in situations calling for flexibility. They tend to take risks and are at ease with people. They can make things happen by bringing action to a concept. Their favorite question would be *If . . .*

❏ **WHY?** It is important for parents and caregivers to see these differences. Language is a facet of autonomy, the ability to self-regulate and self-direct. Language directs our thoughts and actions which encompasses social interactions. However, the emergence of language and speech is a left hemisphere acquisition. The left hemisphere gradually tries to dominate thoughts, actions, and behaviors, and words. Children make up questions and process grammar motivated by the sound of your voice and by the use of new words. By seeing the differences of the two hemispheres our words and actions can design and create activities and language experiences that deploy the strengths of both hemispheres.

Encouraging Language Development with Thoughts and Words

Can you stimulate both hemispheres? Think of playing peek-a-boo! Courtney Cazden (1981) describes playing peek-a-boo as a language game. Playing peek-a-boo with young children stimulates the visual right side of the brain and the verbal left side of the brain. The listening skills and the verbal cues of the simple rhythmic verse, "Peek-a-boo, I see you," merge with the visual dramatization of covering your eyes and then quickly saying, "Boo!"

Read nursery rhymes and storybooks to children that continue to supply visual imagery and verbal cues. A few suggestions are:

> Ahlberg, Janet and Allan. *Peek a Boo!*; *The Jolly Postman*
> Bell, Sara. *Farmyard Families* (A flip-flap book)
> Brown, Marc. *Hand Rhymes*
> Brown, Margaret Wise. *Goodnight Moon; The Little Fur Family*
> Carle, Eric. *Very Hungry Caterpillar*
> Hill, Eric. *Where's Spot?*
> Kelley, True. *Look, Baby! Listen, Baby! Do, Baby!*
> Kurnhardt, Dorothy. *Pat the Bunny*
> Nichol, bp *Once: A Lullaby*
> Slobodkina, Esphyr. *Caps for Sale*
> Watson, Clyde and Wendy. *Catch Me and Kiss Me and Say It Again.*
> Williams, Vera. *"More More More," Said the Baby*
> Wood, Don and Audrey. *The Big Hungry Bear*

Language development can coexist in the left and right hemispheres while reading just about any story to children. The visual imagery procured along with the audiovisual aid of reading aloud allows the mind and body to share the transmission of thoughts and words.

❑ **IF** you peruse a photo album with a child;

❑ **THEN** language development can be mobilized in both the left and right side of the brain. (Especially with pictures about themselves!)

❑ **HOW?** By talking about the scenes or the time of different events captured on film creates a visual image they can recall.

❑ **IF** you utilize the process of baking and cooking with children as a language enhancer, physical accomplishment, and social interaction;

❑ **THEN** a transfer between the two sides can be shared.

❑ **HOW?** By reading the recipe to a child they can follow the sequential order of ingredients. Allowing the child to "measure" and add the ingredients; and by stirring manually or with a mechanical sort of mixer transmits different ways of learning.

Initiate a conversation about favorite foods, the tastiest meal to prepare, or the most delicious dessert to bake together.

Read books about cooking, baking, and eating such as:

Barrett, J. *Cloudy with a Chance of Meatballs*
Carle, Eric. *Very Hungry Caterpillar*
deBrunhoff, Laurent. *Babar Learns to Cook*
Degen, Bruce. *Jamberry*
dePaola, Tomie. *Pancakes for Breakfast;
    Goldilocks and the Three Bears*
Krasilovsky, Phyllis. *The Man Who Cooked for
    Himself*
Lobel, Arnold. *Frog and Toad Are Friends*
McPhail, David. *Party*
Numeroff, Laura Jaffe. *If You Gave a Mouse a
    Cookie*
Polacco, Patricia. *Thundercake*
Dr. Seuss. *Green Eggs and Ham*

Waddell, Martin, and Angela Barrett. *The Hidden House*

Wood, Don and Audrey. *The Big Hungry Bear*

❑ **IF** the left brain fine motor skill of stringing wooden beads is chosen by a child as an activity;

❑ **THEN** the child may create conceptual patterns.

❑ **HOW?** By your encouragement and help in letting them "see" the beads as patterns.

❑ **WHY?** According to Healy (1987) children who organize their information during the sensorimotor stage (put to use their senses with trust, exploration, and language) seem quite capable of organizing, associating, and adding new thoughts, words, and ideas.

■

The Relationship of Innovative Ideas and Creative Thoughts to Language Development

Innovative ideas will sustain creative thoughts along with language development. With the development of language and the onset of left-side dominance, activities and experiences have to be designed that require visual thinking—the . . . close your eyes and imagine . . . type of thinking. "Visual thinking breaks you out of the mindset of language, which keeps you stuck in a certain way of seeing and expressing the world," believes Bob McKim, design professor at Stanford and author of *Thinking Visually* (1980).

With visual thinking, the results are images. To McKim, imagery is more than what your eyes see and your hand can sketch. There is also inner imagery, what you see with your eyes closed. Children can be given opportunities to exercise and strengthen their ability to imagine rather than taking the familiar for granted. One example McKim suggests is to shut your eyes and imagine an apple. What do you see?

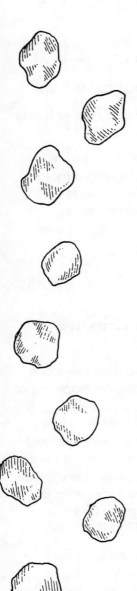

Now visualize holding the crisp, red apple. Feel its weight, size, skin, coolness. Imagine biting into the apple. Hear the crunch? Smell and taste its sweetness. Feelings and senses are intertwined conjuring up a more realistic, three-dimensional image. Problem solving requires this type of thinking. When problems are imagined in such a tangible, seeable way, solutions come to mind with more force, more variety, and more detail. Images provide a rich, expressive medium for thought that complements analytical reasoning and offers quick, unexpected jumps and connections.

❏ **IF** research is claiming that toddlers and preschoolers need to move about, listen, and communicate to think and learn;

❏ **THEN** they need their minds *and* bodies to be in perpetual, perceptual motion. Young children are actively involved in learning what their bodies are capable of doing—jumping, spinning, rolling, or tumbling. They enjoy playing. And they enjoy pretending. So I have used my imagination to design activities that organize these playing and pretending interests and physical capabilities.

❏ **HOW?** Cut up brown paper grocery bags into one dozen large, irregular shapes about the size of dinner plates.

❏ **WHY?** Pretend these are large rocks.

You need to establish an area of a room or yard that can become an imaginary stream of water or a lake. Scatter the "rocks" throughout the "water" not too far apart.

Curiosity is aroused by your actions. As the children gather around tell them you are pretending the area you have designated is now full of water. The brown paper shapes are pretend "rocks" poking out of the water. The object of the game is to *jump* from "rock" to "rock" without falling into the "water."

I have at times called the game Musical Rocks.

❏ **IF** you play lively, spirited music, the children automatically begin to dance, jump, and dive onto the scattered "rocks."

❏ **THEN** stop the music.

❏ **HOW?** Play with music: Everyone jumps and dances from "rock" to "rock." Everyone must jump onto a "rock" when the music stops, or

everyone must swim to a "rock," or

everyone must hop on one foot to a "rock," or

everyone must skip to a "rock."

The children integrate verbal, visual, and physical skills through this activity. This is the same idea as Musical Chairs *except* there are enough "rocks" for everyone!

❏ **WHY?** There is no competition involved. The idea of "no competition" equals no hurt feelings. I make a point of stressing no competition in activities for 2, 3, and 4 year olds because a 2 year old would immediately cry and ask, "Where's mine?" Two year olds learn by observing and imitating the language and behavior of others. So there has to be an equal number of playing pieces in *every* game for a two year old to to able to copy and comprehend the object of a game.

Many 3 and 4 year olds are on the verge of participating and sharing. They are trying to make friends within a group, so there have to be enough playing pieces to encourage 3 and 4 year olds to relate to each other. No one should feel left out. These children are generally ready and willing to cooperate and begin to refine their social behavior. They are entering a socialization threshold.

Over the course of time the children have developed physical skills, enhanced their language skills and social skills and strengthened their imaginations with this simple game:

They have tried to refine their own jumping skills by pretending the "water" is icy cold.

They try their best to stay out of the "water."

They kneel on the "rocks" and pretend to peer into the "water" to see frogs, turtles, or fish.

They have been able to learn and understand the meaning of new words introduced through their play.

They have been able to learn through the use of their body/mind.

Their actions, suggestions, and new ideas have been recognized, affirmed, and approved by me and their peers.

■

Reading Stories for Listening Skills and Visual Images

Children need to reach a balance between energetic activities such as pretend rocks and quiet, passive, though thought-provoking activities. Reading stories aloud offers that balance and helps to establish a sense of closure.

❏ **IF** after playing such an active game, children need to rest and regroup;

❏ **THEN** I would read stories, particularly stories about water, rocks, fish, and alligators:

Hutchins, Pat. *Changes, Changes*
Lionni, Leo. *Swimmy*
McCloskey, Robert. *Make Way for Ducklings*
Sendak, Maurice. *Alligators all Around*
Steig, William. *Sylvester and the Magic Pebble*
Waber, Bernard. *Lyle, Lyle Crocodile: The House of East 88th Street*
Yashima, Taro. *Umbrella*

❏ **HOW?** Borrow from the library. In many libraries, in the chidren's department, there is a Parent/Teacher Reference section. Here you can find books solely devoted to children's literature that help make

your reading selections meaningful, informative, and enjoyable for the children.

Discuss water, fish, rocks, alligators, or ducks with the children and ask if they might have a book you could borrow to share and extend the activity. Describe the daily activities to each child's parent or guardian and encourage them to read to the child.

❏ **WHY?** Giving children a chance to relax by hearing a story offers valuable self-regulatory development.

Reading stories provides a chance to synthesize or put together their thoughts and actions derived from their daily activities.

Reading stories expands the imagination as they visualize the characters and situations they are hearing.

After reading a story exchange ideas, encourage children to talk about their favorite character, the story's sequence, the most interesting part, and the final outcome. Encourage children to ask questions. Explain why particular situations occurred. Make analogies between the story and an aspect of their lives. Ask questions! Promote inquisitiveness! "Could that ever really happen to you?" Ask the children, "What would you do if such a thing did happen?" The give and take of asking questions and seeking answers fosters listening and thinking skills. Helping children learn to listen is an essential factor furthering their cognitive growth. This give and take of questions and answers elicits thoughts which quite effectively develops and includes the properties of language.

Reading stories to children enhances the interplay of their thoughts, actions, and words.

Reading stories is sharing time and sharing time together imbues the greater value of trust.

Maintaining Innovative Ideas

Have you ever stopped to think where and how do you get your ideas? We've just looked at how clinical and experimental research gives evidence on how they're processed, but where did they come from? (Close your eyes to think about it.) Many of my own ideas come from reading, observing, listening, and copying styles, words, and thoughts that impress me most. The same holds true for children. Mental patterns and word associations become concrete when children's ideas, actions, behaviors, methods of expression, and participation skills can be accepted, verbally recognized, and praised.

So provoke innovative ideas. Teach new words. Read, listen, and communicate. You promote the properties of language development. As a result, you can generate extraordinary outcomes.

Chapter 4

Active Learning to Pull It All Together

■

The Importance of Active Learning

For children to think and learn, act upon and acquire language from their environment, trust and exploratory behavior are essential. Pretend play, puppets, acting out dramatic situations, and reading stories are a few developmentally appropriate early childhood forms of play essential for two year olds and preschoolers to learn language development, concept formation, and social growth. Each time a child's physical abilities increase, their perceptual world widens.

Let's look at examples of active learning at *every* stage of development where the more children learn about their bodies the more their minds can absorb.

Infants who can sit now demonstrate control over abdominal muscles. Even more importantly they have free hands to experience grasping, poking, turning, dropping, and throwing. Each activity in itself causes an effect.

Toddlers discover the world by chewing, touching, banging, listening, and disassembling. Physical contact with trusted caregivers promotes the potential for learning cause and effect: touching can bring a smile, reaching out can symbolize pick me up, tugging always gets your attention. Children learn early to register a connection between their actions and the clear effects they have on the people comprising their world. Such effects teach them whom to seek out and whom to avoid. The language that is soon to accompany these children is the culmination of honing their listening skills into interpretations of your actions and reactions.

Children from 2 1/2 through 5 years of age learn to pretend, imagine, step back, and even look at themselves in relation to their actions. Early explorations and discoveries lead to their more complex forms of play. Children can not come to know about people, places, and things if they have not had opportunities to think about them and actively deal and learn from them. And the more varied and frequent we make these dealings the more concepts we help children come to understand through the combined effort of physical and intellectual skills. The children discover and learn through the body and the mind or the body:mind.

■

Active Learning: A Holistic Approach

Integrating the merits of play with dramatic-characteristic situations enhances a child's curiosity thereby increasing their receptiveness to listen and understand more words and actions. Through their words, actions, and ideas children learn to ask questions, seek possible solutions, develop the properties of language, and attain problem-solving skills. Active holistic learning is children putting their thoughts into actions. Their thoughts hold memory meaning (knowledge) and they understand how to apply this knowledge in their behavior and play. Active learning holistically is a child developing physical, intellectual, social, emotional, and intuitive skills. The children learn "what feels right."

❏ **IF** the motive for pretend play, for example, is for the child to act out their relationship and meaning of various people, actions, and settings they are familiar with;

❏ **THEN** they need to have attentive parents and child-care workers to provide ways of supporting and nourishing their ideas.

❑ **HOW?** Some activities you can plan and structure if you have an idea or experiment you want to introduce to your group. However, be sure it is of interest to your group first. Don't set yourself up for frustration. Remember too that these activities have to be developmentally appropriate. They have to suit the interest, physical capabilities, and comprehension levels of the children involved.

Let me set the stage with this example of how I have asked questions and offered suggestions to help my group become more aware of possibilities in their play.

A few of the children were playing with the Fisher-Price® people playhouse. I sat and listened, respecting their choice of play, and then asked a few questions about the "family" in the playhouse. The children had already assumed different roles with the playhouse people. I asked the "father" (three year old Mark) if he had ever taken his "family" fishing at the lake. "Father" Mark said, "No." But his "family" heard the question and they wanted to go! So we all went fishing.

The "family" included: 20 month old Tyler; 2 year old Matthew; 3 year olds Mark, Kate, and Candace; 4 year old Tim; and 5 year old Joseph.

For this water play activity:

> I filled a baby bathtub halfway with warm water (to represent the lake).
> I set the tub on a low, small table indoors (go directly outdoors on a warm day).
> We collected all of the Fisher-Price® people.
> We found bath toy boats and I provided square Tupperware® containers so each child would have a boat for their plastic people to float in on the lake.

Are you using your imagination to visualize this activity? The children sure did! Their "families" could fish, swim, and dive into the "lake." They even

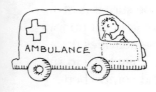

decided to have a picnic on the banks of this "lake." (Now you have a new setting for snacktime—around the water table.) After the picnic, to dramatize the scene, I told them to be careful because a storm cloud was approaching. They boarded their "families" back on their boats. I rocked the tub to purposely cause havoc. Some boats capsized, so the children eagerly worked at a rescue. They were enthusiastic to assume new roles. They needed lifeguards and rescue workers to swim out and save the people.

The actions and language of the older children directly influenced and taught the younger children in the group (as in all daily activities) new concepts and words. They worked together to push the floating capsized boats over to the people. (I was delighted to see them using their minds to solve such a dilemma!) They were totally absorbed in their "work"/play. The rescue workers even yelled out to the "people" to "Hold on!"

They threw popsicle sticks in the water (more floating devices) to help save the "people." Mark and Tim ran to get toy helicopters and airplanes to airlift the people out of the water. They decided some of the people needed to go to the hospital. The Fisher-Price® playhouse immediately transformed into a hospital. On their own initiative they again knew they needed to assume new roles—doctors, nurses, ambulance drivers. I recognized their interests by suggesting additional props; reassured their actions by explaining possible consequences; and affirmed their creative thoughts, thinking processes, and wonderful participation within the group.

❏ **WHY?** Active learning involves movement, listening, thinking, and understanding the many concepts and new words one activity can produce. Active learning comes through the energy children use to *see*. Seeing what floats, what sinks, observing each other's behavior, imagining their pretend story and visualizing their actions within that story. They are actively learning listening skills. Children *hear* each other describe their scene, consequences, outcomes.

They are listening to my questions and suggestions. They hear my encouragement. Remember children learn through their senses. They are also *touching/feeling* the water, the "people," the props used to create each new scene/concept. The emotional affective learning is promoted by their actions—fishing, swimming, and diving happily; the need to assist in the rescue; the feelings expressed while pretending to swim, fly an airplane or helicopter, drive an ambulance, or save the life of another person.

Active learning integrates pretend play acting and story telling.

❏ **IF** you read a story such as:

> Aardema, Verna. *Who's In Rabbit's House?*
> Eastman, P. D. *Are You My Mother?*
> Ets, Marie. *The Elephant in the Well*
> Martin, Bill, Jr. *Brown Bear, Brown Bear, What Do You See?*
> Sadler, Marilyn. *It's Not Easy Being a Bunny;*

❏ **THEN** gather stuffed animals, figures and toys that match the characters (bears, bunnies, elephants, birds) and objects (trucks, cars, planes, steamshovels) in the story.

❏ **HOW?** Read the story. Afterwards ask the children questions about the story, "What was your favorite character?", "Which part of the story did you like the best?", "How do you think . . . felt in that part of the story?", "How did . . . make *you* feel?"

Collect all of the animals and objects you have gathered that correspond to the story and ask the children to select the figure or object they would like to pretend to be. Read the first page again and let the children pretending to be those animals and objects act out what is on that page. Read page by page as the children act out the events and situations on each page.

❏ **WHY?** You have to feel comfortable in the world of children's books. Preparing a story for the children to act out allows you to see the children enjoy stories and books. Studies have proven that children who are introduced to books as babies and who are read to frequently and encouraged to think and talk about the pictures, characters, and situations they meet in books become good readers. Children learn to read because adults have provided a positive attitude toward reading and books. As we observe and learn and grow in tune with a child's development we must assist with their visual and verbal cues to help affective/emotional growth connect with their cognitive/intellectual changes. With our help children see books as an adventure to be explored, a treasure to be discovered.

So how *do* children think, learn, and act? Through their play. Dramatic pretend play is only one aspect of childrens' play that helps them:

> develop creative thoughts,
>
> have opportunities to talk and listen,
>
> hear questions and answers, and
>
> learn new concepts, new words, deal with fears, and solve problems.

■

Active Learning = Child Power

Do you know what is one of the most difficult things parents and child-care workers have to learn? To permit the child to be the "leader" or "signal giver." We have to learn to accept and respect child power where we take the learning initiative from the child. We often think we know what children should be doing, should be learning. If children think and learn by doing then we have to learn to follow their lead. Experiences for children have no meaning without *children* doing the experiencing. With our help recognizing childrens' physical capabilities and intellectual maturity we can promote and provoke learning with activities generated from the children's interests. Children do not need someone to tell them what to do, how to experience—we have been encouraging them to think and do on their own since birth! What they need from us is established, consistent expectations of behavior that recognize, encourage, reassure, and affirm their positive behavior. Children still need to think and do with their own minds and bodies.

Dr. T. Berry Brazelton and his associates (1974) say that children need adults to recognize and encourage an independent search for environmental cues and games—the child's own feeling of competence and of voluntary control is strengthened. The primary task of childhood is to be socialized into becoming an active and productive member of their families and of society. We help children develop this task by offering suitable activities that allow them to imagine and pretend they are active and productive members of their families and society.

■

Why We Pull It All Together with Play

A synopsis of the radical thesis on the character of play of Johann Huzinga (1955) is presented in the book, *Understanding Children's Play*. Huzinga argued that society is generated by the same formative processes that generate play. Play is a way for children to grow in individual and social areas. Play is valued as a means for children to work out their difficulties. In doing so they learn to meet the challenges of the world with confidence. All of their pretend play, full of symbolic meaning, relates to a child's playful, familiar world. The thinking skills, listening skills, language development, and ways children express their emotions through play, eventually connect to the real world they must learn to function in as active and productive members of their families and society.

Active Learning and Self-Discovery Through Block Building

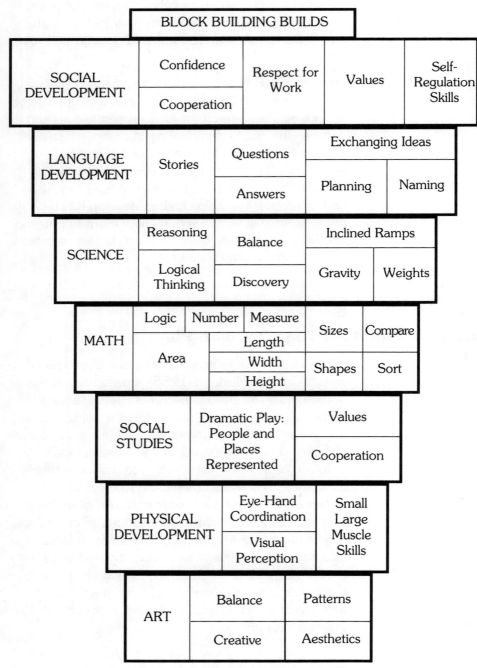

BLOCK BUILDING BUILDS

SOCIAL DEVELOPMENT	Confidence	Respect for Work	Values	Self-Regulation Skills
	Cooperation			

LANGUAGE DEVELOPMENT	Stories	Questions	Exchanging Ideas	
		Answers	Planning	Naming

SCIENCE	Reasoning	Balance	Inclined Ramps	
	Logical Thinking	Discovery	Gravity	Weights

MATH	Logic	Number	Measure	Sizes	Compare
	Area		Length		
			Width	Shapes	Sort
			Height		

SOCIAL STUDIES	Dramatic Play: People and Places Represented	Values
		Cooperation

PHYSICAL DEVELOPMENT	Eye-Hand Coordination	Small Large Muscle Skills
	Visual Perception	

ART	Balance	Patterns
	Creative	Aesthetics

Block Building

Building with blocks uses all disciplines that help children actively learn. Since humans learn through all senses simultaneously, it is important to develop all aspects of development through play. The water play, digging in dirt and sand, nature walks, reconstructing discarded appliance boxes, and the housekeeping corner are educationally sound examples of play that allow children to learn about their lives and the world around them. Information has been gathered through the sense of sight, hearing, taste, touch, and smell; and has been processed through internal efforts, tensions, and emotions. To be able to integrate new ideas and actions into successful ventures children need to be exposed to language and experiences which stimulate provocative thoughts. Familiarity bathed in encouragement piques curious minds to seek new experiences and feats. Learning occurs when children relate to past experiences, affecting a deeper understanding when they undertake new tasks.

For all children block building integrates the physical, social, emotional, and intellectual development in three-dimensional boldness. Block building allows children to think mathematically, scientifically, and aesthetically while using concrete play things:

• Through block building children build language skills. They construct their buildings from simple ideas into complex masterpieces. Playing with blocks provides the satisfaction of getting a job done.

• Block building as a developmentally appropriate physical activity allows children to develop both large and small muscle coordination. Playing with blocks strengthens eye-hand coordination using skills of balance and control.

• Children can learn the social value of respecting each others work through any block building activity. Within a group, children feel the satisfaction of being a member—that good feeling of cooperating and belonging to the group. Working within a group built upon this feeling, fosters a responsibility to yourself and to your work, along with a social responsibility to the group.

• The amount of work and play involved in building with blocks builds self-esteem. The work of each child is of sheer creative effort. The simplicity of the basic units involved with this activity requires dramatic and imaginative thoughts that may symbolize real-life situations. Being engrossed in imaginative play blocks out tension.

• Emotionally, imagination, persistence, and patience are the basic building blocks required for children to learn to enjoy and appreciate their efforts. With persistence and patience children learn to accept some degree of emotional frustration because they know the end result is their mastery of design and functional use. Independent play and group play teaches a child, without being aware of it, the habits most needed for intellectual growth, such as persistence, which is so important in all aspects of learning. Perseverance is easily acquired around enjoyable activities such as chosen play. Learning to persevere at an early age with enjoyable tasks through play helps develop the habit of seeing an activity or project through to completion. This is a very useful tool for the very near future of school.

• To be considered intelligent, children need some degree of physical ability and intuitional awareness. Children need to learn to like and respect themselves as well as feel comfortable socially within a group. Children need to learn to express their emotions creatively and diplomatically to make their needs and wants known. Working with blocks builds this fundamental foundation and provides a framework of intellectual architecture. Intellectually, children need to understand cause and effect relationships; how to structure their thinking to be able to solve problems and get a job done. Intellect can be developed using these concrete unit blocks that involve mathematical concepts such as one-to-one correspondence, sorting, fitting together, counting, matching, comparing, seeing spatial relationships, and seeing and handling fractional parts that can make up a concrete whole.

• Scientifically and aesthetically, the control, balance, and stability of block building relates to our life-long functions that involve logical thinking. Think about when you pack groceries either in the grocery bags at the supermarket or into your own kitchen cabinets. Isn't that a feat in itself? How about delivery people or cargo carriers loading their trucks and equipment in such a way that enables them to locate their products logically?

We can learn early that various shapes and sizes can fit together within a space dependent on our skills of balance and stability. Block building therefore provides children a solid foundation for gathering information, becoming active learners, and in turn for "building" productive thinkers.

■

A Self-Analysis Promotes Active Learning

Being creative means you can invent, imagine, make plans, move around, discuss and solve problems. To know and believe in yourself and your ideas allows you to believe in the ideas of a child. From your own creativity and understanding of child development you can allow children to try out their own ideas and promote in them constant active learning.

For children, play is the source where information has been gathered and processed through their senses, motor abilities, and the language used within and about their environment. The young children in your care use the playful manipulation of toys, people, and objects in their environment to acquire information about the world and lives they will have to assume.

Naturalist Gerald Durrell (1988) observes that "all of

us are born with an interest in the world around us. Watch a human baby or any other young animal looking or crawling about. It is investigating and learning things with all its' senses of sight, hearing, taste, touch and smell. From the moment we are born we are explorers in a complex and fascinating world."

For some unfortunately, discoveries may be limited and even fade with a dull environment or over time from the harsh pressures they must face in their young lives. Children lucky enough to be cared for by sensitive, considerate, and respectable caregivers like you can keep this interest alive. You can motivate children's interest to explore and learn by making your environment stimulating, your language appropriate, and the activities developmentally suitable for them. If you can get them into the habit of acquiring information and skills through playing, imitating, exploring, listening, and remembering; then subsequently achievements through discovery should continue to motivate their interest to explore and learn throughout their lives.

■

Our Participation Facilitates Active Learning

Making life easier for a child enhances their love, trust, and openness to accept and learn from you. We make a child's life easier by the tone we set: a stimulating keen enthusiasm or a frenzied bedlam. Offering comfort to allay fears during a thunderstorm facilitates a child's life. Understanding a child's hurt feelings, accepting their questions and answers, acknowledging one's good behavior are ways that help children learn you are also a participant. Figuratively speaking, children learn that we are all on the same team.

Letting children use play to learn about art, music, science, and math helps them focus on learning through self-discovery with the people and the resources in their environment. Simple experiences create simple schemes. Children are naturally inquisitive. If what may seem so incomprehensible is presented in a simplified fashion these simple schemes amplify learning. Facilitating active learning for young children includes our participation in dealing with their questions, feelings, reactions, exchanges of ideas, stories, and respect.

Facilitation and our participation encourages language development. We provide suggestions, more questions, plans, more stories, values, and ideas. Introducing young children to innovative ideas with gentle guidance and encouragement gives them opportunities to grasp and understand novel, playful experiences. Think of your participation as a means of pulling it all together.

PART TWO

Art and Creative Thinking

Chapter 5

Art For the Child's Sake

■

The Value of Art

❏ **IF** you view the Meaning of Life as an integrated whole not simply intellectual, but both physical and emotional as well;

❏ **THEN** as a parent or child-care provider you can influence the whole child—physically, intellectually, socially, and emotionally.

❏ **HOW?** By providing activities children have to think about, do independently, or do cooperatively within a group and feel free to playfully pretend. My group might be busy building wooden or cardboard houses, pretending to be electricians wiring those houses, operating their own stores, going on trips, planting flower bulbs, or making bird feeders. We often listen to stories, "write" stories, produce plays, bake special treats, perform community services, and draw.

❏ **WHY?** Is there enough emphasis on creativity and self-expression for young children? Are needs being met through art and play? The experiences involved in the "making of" and the "appreciation of" art offers affective/emotional growth as well as cognitive/intellectual skills. The value of offering creative activities to children aims at holistic development:

imagination,
self-expression,
sensory experiences,
satisfaction and enjoyment,
emotional release,
good work habits,

learning experiences,
thinking skills and concentration,
language skills,
eye-hand coordination,
harmony, rhythm, and balance,
gross and fine motor skills,
friendships, and
insight into one's own feelings.

Theoretically, creativity appears to involve understanding, flexibility, originality, and divergent thinking. This means if you and the children are creative you see opportunities that change the things that are, spark new ideas, and see ways to invent new or different things. According to Howard Gardner (1980) an art experience can help children to see "new relationships between previously unrelated objects or ideas."

Art offers children opportunities for self-expression and individualism. Art experiences are emotionally satisfying for most children because they learn to feel good about themselves when we give their work a well deserved affirmation for creative and artistic effort.

■

Developmental Art

Children refine their skills and development in eye-hand coordination through their art materials. It is important, however, that we do not push children in their development. They set their own pace. Our responsibility is to recognize individual development and provide appropriate activities.

Scribbling: The First Developmental Stage of Art

Young children in your care, starting at approximately eighteen months, with or without language, can benefit from an art experience. Often, with very young children things just happen to them, they have no say or choice in the matter. For instance, they get fed and bathed when we deem necessary; we take them to the pediatrician for a check-up. Young children only see and feel what has been done to them. They are too young to understand why it must be done. And they have limited ways of expressing how they feel, besides crying.

❏ **IF** you have very young children in your care and you are planning an art activity;

❏ **THEN** include those youngsters also. One of the first ways children learn to express themselves is through movement. Between eighteen months and 2-1/2 years old, depending on the child, when given a few crayons and a blank piece of paper the child will scribble on the paper. Over the next few months, with increased coordination, and frequent experiences with crayons, children realize they are producing these motions on their paper. They are learning cause and effect.

Coloring: Coordination and Creativity vs. Coloring Books

The scribbling stage lasts from two to four years. Given early scribbling opportunities and with the child's own maturity, they discover they can control their motions. Controlling their motions gives satisfaction and confidence and a new way of expressing themselves. Again you have to use your best judgment in deciding when to introduce crayons. As with any activity talk, explain, and demonstrate the use for every child. I recall a group of 3 and 4 year olds gathering around the table to draw and color with crayons. There was an eighteen month old child who followed along wanting to participate. He understood what the others were going to do and could only say, "Color." He had "colored" with the group before. I automatically picked him up and put him in a high chair to be a part of the group at the table. But I did this silently. I handed him a crayon from the tray of crayons on the table and turned away to get him a piece of paper. While my back was turned, he ate the crayon! I should have been talking to him, reminding him it was time to color, telling him, "Here is your crayon," and explaining I had to get him paper. His immediate observation, however, was associating the high chair with food! So remember to recognize what a child is about to do; reaffirm their actions and offer your approval—with your actions and words.

I also think crayons look tempting to a child. They are colorful and look chewable. Remember that children from birth to 1-1/2 to 2 years old are still in the sensorimotor stage of developmentally learning through their senses and body movements. We, as adults, do the same type of learning with sensory stimulation without even realizing it. How often do you find yourself writing while chewing the top of your pen or pencil? Can you sit still—without wiggling your foot or touching your face during a conversation when it is your turn to listen? While we are using one sense to learn and understand something we involuntarily use another sense to reinforce what we are trying to absorb. We are learning with our minds and bodies in motion; the body:mind.

I have had parents come in and say, "I'm glad he/ she (their child) comes *here* (my home) for artwork, I don't allow it in my house. I'm afraid they'll write on the walls!" That's unfortunate for both the young child and the parents. Scribbling means enjoyment, happiness, release, and the gaining of an important function—the coordination of motions.

❑ **HOW?** Your actions and words are the most effective ways to prevent children from scribbling on walls. Demonstrate that the crayon colors on a piece of paper. Affirm their actions: "You are doing a good job coloring on your paper!" "I like the way you colored your picture!"

Approve their actions while the children are coloring, "Look at all of the color on your paper!" Your words of affirmation and approval reveal what you expect and accept of the children.

I have also avoided buying soap crayons—the crayons children are given to use in the bathtub because it washes off. Can young children make such a fine discrimination between a washable, tiled surface or a painted, Sheetrock wall? Should they have to? Provide the right atmosphere and talk about your rules, "Crayons (paints, markers, glue . . .) stay at the table."

Children should not be forced to do artwork nor be forced to finish their work within a specific time frame. Sometimes, just like adults, they need a minute or two to walk away, collect their thoughts, and then return to their work. If they walk away with a crayon or paintbrush in their hand remind them to leave it on the table *before* leaving the room. The proper material, the proper space, and the proper atmosphere should provide a sufficient outlet so the need or desire to scribble on walls is not necessary. You want the children to feel happy within the group. In order to do so they can and should learn to comply with "house rules."

❑ **WHY?** The scribbling stage usually lasts from two to four years. The main needs of children during this stage are to satisfy the desire for movement and to learn to control movement. They are learning the principle of cause and effect through their own actions. This same principle applies to other facets of development the children are learning, not just in art. Gaining control of movements with repeated experiences allows children to discover when they can walk without assistance, or speak their first words, or learn to eat by themselves. We can't force a child to eat neatly and properly when the control and coordination of their movements has not yet been developed. It would be unfair to scold a child for making a mess while eating if their coordination is not yet developed. They are trying to learn on their own. The same is true with scribbling. Their artwork may look messy to you, that's insignificant; they are gaining control of their motions. It would be unfair to interfere with a child's learning by imposing an aesthetic value other than the child's.

Coloring books also tend to impose a value on a child other than their own and therefore interfere with this same type of learning. Children have to learn to coordinate their own motions on paper and not be confronted with the task of following the outlines of someone else. Coloring books prevent children from creating their own relationship with their artwork. Coloring books leave no opportunity for children to express their own feelings of happiness or frustration or their own ideas.

According to Victor D'Amico (1953) "It has been proven by experimentation and research that more than half of all children, once exposed to coloring books, lose their creativeness and their independence of expression, and become rigid and dependent." You may logically think coloring books improve a child's fine motor skills by developing the discipline of staying within the lines, but in actuality this is not true at all. If children draw a picture it therefore becomes their own creation. They have developed their own sense of incentive to color their picture as they see it. Children give meaning to the person or object in their picture according to their own relationship with it. Therefore they assert more effort to draw and color within their own boundaries. Children's urge to do the right thing grows out of learning about their own capabilities. Our job is to help them think and learn and do for themselves. We must ask children what they need, what they want, what they think, what they want to do, and then provide answers and activities that meet those needs. We do not help children by doing the thinking and learning for them. By this I mean children's art expression has to be their own expression.

❏ **IF** a child asks to draw;

❏ **THEN** we provide crayons, paper, and encouragement.

❏ **IF** a child says, "I don't know what to draw";

❏ **THEN** we can offer them suggestions.

❏ **HOW?** Suggest they draw someone in their family, something about their house, something they like to do, or how they feel. But we can not draw it for them!

❏ **WHY?** If you show a child "how to draw" you are imposing your imagination and any artistic skills you may have onto that child. The drawing becomes your expression not the child's. Let's say, for example, the child decides to draw a dog—your neighbor's playful, spunky dog. If the dog is outdoors when the children are out, this child may enjoy petting the dog or chasing the dog. The child has developed his/her own personal view and relationship with this dog. You on the other hand may also enjoy petting and even chasing the dog but your relationship may be a little more reserved because you are also thinking about this child's safety and attending to what the other children in your group are doing outdoors. You have an entirely different concept of the same dog as compared to that of the child's. Also with your drawing skills you set a standard. Children think their dog has to look like yours, so instead of "helping" the child you interfere with their own creative expression and shake their confidence.

Remember as well that a young child of 1-1/2 to 2-1/2 years old is still trying to control scribbling motions. So even if they tell you they have drawn a dog often you will be hard pressed to find it! The point is they see the dog in their drawing and they are confident and happy about their artwork.

■

Art Develops Language and Creative Thought

Coloring, drawing, painting, or any means of creative expression are excellent avenues for us to use to stimulate language development. Three and four year old children begin to label their scribblings because they are connecting mental images to their artwork. They may draw round circles for heads and bodies and add long lines for arms and legs. This shows us the children are thinking and making connections to their social and emotional world through their drawings. Encourage children to talk about their drawings—and accept what they tell you! You can also encourage children to make pictures in their minds by asking questions about their drawing.

Three year old Kate, working with purple Cray Pas, excitedly asks me to look at the cat she drew. I see a little purple squiggle on the left hand side of her paper with a vague resemblance of a cat. She is so enthusiastic. I say, "That is a beautiful cat. Is it your cat?" Kate says, "No, it belongs to these people." She promptly chooses another color and busily creates an entire group of squiggle people. She says, "It was lost and they are bringing it home." She encircles the entire scene with full, round circles and calls these circles their home.

This change, from scribbling motions to thinking in terms of pictures, is a major development. From now on Kate's thinking will be in terms of mental images she has formed from her own experiences, concepts, and relationships. Children are making a chapter in their life's history every time they "do art" because they apply previously stored information to each new creation. Observing these changes in each child's level of thinking allows you to add new facets of information, different suggestions, and interesting questions.

I was lucky when Kate asked me to look at the "cat" she had drawn. That was a big clue to help me ask questions about her drawing and encourage Kate to talk about her picture. Some children enjoy the confidence of doing artwork but lack the confidence to talk about their art.

❑ **IF** you have children who do not communicate feelings well through verbal language;

❑ **THEN** they can and should be encouraged to talk about their artwork.

❑ **HOW?** Comment positively about childrens' lines or shapes. Tell them how you like the colors they used or the movements they make on their paper. You can ask, "What is happening here?" (Point to one section of the picture to stimulate discussion.)

❑ **WHY?** It is important for children to develop a balance between thinking and feeling. By talking about their art, children become more sensitive to your encouragement and more aware of their art materials and their abilities to use them.

■

Giving Praise

Praise a child's artwork, and their actions, when the child deserves your praise.

❑ **IF** a child is eagerly making art and talking about their artwork or feelings;

❑ **THEN** they are thinking creatively and deserve your praise.

❑ **IF** you are working with a child who is reluctant to talk about their artwork and through your questions and encouragement the child opens up;

❑ **THEN** that child deserves your praise. Your praise should build the child's confidence to draw and speak.

❑ **IF** you single out one particular style of drawing a child may use because you like it;

❑ **THEN** this may create the harmful effect of limiting the child's creative experimentation with other styles of drawing.

❑ **HOW?** By singling one style of art out of a child's entire drawing process.

❑ **WHY?** By decorating a wall or a refrigerator with only one style of art per child, you create that feeling of meeting a standard. Accept *all* forms of children's art expression. By selecting one style, you limit experimentation by creating a feeling within a child that that particular style must be copied to please you.

Remember that children need to engage in creative activities to express themselves not to just produce a picture.

❑ **IF** there is no reason to praise a child's work or actions;

❑ **THEN** don't.

❑ **HOW?** It is difficult to know when to give praise and when not to give praise to children. When you see them thinking and concentrating on their work they deserve your praise. When they ask questions and when they respond to your questions, when they think and talk about details and feelings associated with their art, they deserve your praise.

❑ **WHY?** If you give praise to children not really applying themselves to their work or play, they seem to know they don't deserve it. False praise destroys a child's confidence in you.

Avoiding Criticism

When children enjoy art activities they are re-creating relationships with people, events, thoughts, and experiences that have held meaning for them. Criticizing a child's artwork actually attacks the significant meaning of those relationships the child is trying to express.

❏ **IF** children use art materials to express their feelings and relationships to people, events, their thoughts and experiences;

❏ **THEN** they can only express themselves at their own level of development. We have to accept each child's level of growth and development. Our encouragement—not criticism—allows children to learn that not everyone will have the same answer or response in order to do excellent work. It is important for us to relate childrens' thinking of what they've seen, talked about, and shown an interest in to their art.

❏ **HOW?** By not expecting to see reality within a child's art. The reality is there for children—it is their way of expressing it. To criticize them because their artwork does not look like what they are telling you it is, undermines creative thoughts.

❏ **WHY?** Criticism can not change a child's level of development. Criticism instead discourages progress and development by weakening a child's confidence. Artwork offers a perfect premise for us to enrich and encourage individual thoughts. We need to recognize and accept each level of development and affirm each child's own special qualities.

Chapter 6

Creative Play: A Hands-On Approach

■

Providing the Right Materials at the Right Time

Crayons span all ages. Be choosy when purchasing crayons. Quality matters more than price. Young children scribbling and three and four year olds drawing are familiarizing themselves with color as well as coordination.

❏ **IF** there is too much wax in the crayon;

❏ **THEN** the color peels up off the paper as the children scribble and draw. So what good is scribbling and drawing if your work does not adhere to your paper?

❏ **IF** your 3 and 4 year olds like to mix colors;

❏ **THEN** experiment to make a new color.

❏ **HOW?** Color a small area with blue and add a layer of yellow over it. You should see a good amount of green. Again, check to see if the color peels off. Colors should mix and produce a new clear color.

❏ **IF** you peel the paper off of each crayon and break them in half;

❏ **THEN** you are making the crayon easier for little fingers to handle.

❏ **HOW?** Just peel and break in half.

❏ **WHY?** The smaller piece allows for a more comfortable feel for the children to express themselves. Children learn early that thin crayons break easily.

This knowledge may restrict their movements causing a careful, timid approach to coloring. Peeling the crayons also gives children creative options such as:

lying the crayon down flat on the paper to produce broad strokes,

drawing with the pointed end, and

drawing with the blunt end.

Creative expression and art experiences are necessary for the healthy growth of all children.

Another inexpensive art medium that can be enjoyed by little ones in your care as well as the older children is Cray Pas. A box of sixteen sticks costs less than $2.00. I offer these oil pastel coloring sticks to the very young children (18 months to 2-1/2 years) because the colors are so bright and work well with very little pressure applied. This allows for more freedom of movement. A lot of color is produced when children draw with Cray Pas. Their pictures are bold and beautiful.

■

Why Play-Doh®, Plasticine, and Plaster?

Why are mud pies and soggy sand cakes so much fun to make? Basically for the same reasons children enjoy Play-Doh® and modeling clay. All of this messy business satisfies very important urges. Remember that at this age children are learning new things through their senses, their bodies, and their movements.

There are three stages of child development characterized through childrens' artwork. During the first stage, at about 2 1/2 to 3 years old, the manipulation of clay allows them to play and learn by squeezing the clay, pulling pieces apart, and pounding it. Clay allows children to learn to use their muscles. Playing with clay satisfies their need to learn through the sense of touch. Clay also satisfies emotional impulses. Pounding clay releases tension, while squeezing it to ooze between the fingers or stretching it to it's breaking point releases inner feelings.

Clay offers children a sense of power—the power to form one shape and then change that shape as often as they like. Children learn they can invent and reinvent, create and re-create.

In the second stage, 3 and 4 year olds enter an exploratory mode where experimenting with clay leads to discovering how to make strips, coils, pellets, and forms which may seem meaningless to you but eventually connects to the experiences that hold meaning for the children. Children playing with clay allows you an additional means of observing and understanding a child's thoughts, feelings, and movements. You can observe their progress from scribble drawing to increased control of producing motions and watch their playful manipulation of clay transform into objects and shapes. Our task is to recognize and accept each stage of their development and offer our encouragement and approval to help build more concepts within the children and more sensitive relationships with those concepts.

During the final, third stage, between 5 and 6 years old, children realize they have the capacity to use clay to mold forms and satisfy the need to express themselves. At this point they incorporate all stages of developmental art.

❏ **IF** you value art for the sake of the children;

❏ **THEN** by providing children with an art medium, such as clay, you are providing opportunities for them to develop thinking skills, language skills, physical skills, and problem-solving skills, as well as aesthetic understanding and values.

Using Play-Doh® and Plasticine Modeling Clay

Modeling is the process of building up a conceived form. For little hands, Play-Doh® is easily molded and manipulated into various shapes. Working with Play-Doh® or clay lets children develop the ability to control and coordinate thinking and motions. For children, 2 1/2 to 4 years old, I offer Play-Doh® or clay to them to enjoy the direct sensory experience of manipulating their lump of dough. They require little incentive; the children get right to work molding and building. Play-Doh® and clay in their hands at this age aids imagination. Remember the little shapes and objects they mold and create hold meaning for them. They are developing their muscles and using their minds to play and pretend. As young as they are they require little assistance from me. I am available only to facilitate and encourage imaginative play.

If one child chooses to play with Play-Doh® or clay they will easily draw a crowd. One afternoon a gathering of four children, ages 2 1/2 to 3 1/2, decided it was Jenny's birthday. Three year old Kate decided she would operate a bakery using Play-Doh®. She busily filled toy pans and cupcake tins to "bake" Play-Doh® cookies and cupcakes for Jenny's party. Two year old Matthew and three year old Candace pretended to be Jenny's parents. Candace and Matthew pretended to drive Jenny to Kate's bakery. They bought Kate's "baked goods" and of course invited Kate to the birthday party. At this point I gave them a box of birthday candles and plastic knives to encourage and affirm their choice of pretend play. This simple art activity encompassed every value an art activity aims at developing.

Play-Doh® can be easily molded and manipulated to fit into commercial products that press and form shapes for you, such as cookie cutters, The Play-Doh® Factory, or animal-shaped molds. Remember we want to see 2 to 4 year old children progress naturally through the three developmental stages of art (the manipulatory stage, the exploratory stage, and the use of design). For this young set, using commercial products lessens their direct manipulation of the Play-Doh® and leaves little need for exploration because the form or shape is created for them, leaving them with a design.

Older children, 5 and 6 year olds, have different needs. Play-Doh® molds and cookie cutters can serve to represent their ideas. Their modeling skills are already somewhat refined. Play-Doh® molds and cookie cutters satisfy their need to express themselves through design. They use the recognizable forms of the molds to express their ideas.

The older children sometimes request the bag of commercial products (animal shapes such as fish, dogs, and dinosaurs, or stars, circles, bottle caps, and so on) for an actual representation of their ideas. By doing so they are changing the art activity into a re-creation of an idea or experience, perhaps a recent visit to an aquarium, the zoo, or the veterinarian's office. The older children in my program have had time to organize their thoughts. They are encouraged to use their imaginations and take plenty of opportunities to refine their artwork. Five and six year olds work spontaneously. Their own ideas and imaginations serve as inspiration.

Modeling clay unlike Play-Doh® is used solely with the hands, at every age, so as not to detract from the sensory experience. Plastic knives are available, if necessary to define and to cut away excess clay to create the desired, conceived form.

■

Sculpture by Plaster of Paris

Introducing the children to Plaster of Paris proved to be one of those ideal, tremendously self-absorbing art activities for each child.

The first step was to give each child a small plastic container of dry Plaster of Paris. I helped them pour in drops of cold water as they watched and stirred the powder into a pliable consistency. At this point we had to decide whether to add more powder or only drops of water until we had the plaster as thick as cookie or bread dough. Then it was ready to be molded into a sculptured form. (I had worked with the plaster prior to the childrens' use so I could understand and explain its properties and what they were experiencing.) They each had large sections of wax paper for their work space. Plaster is tremendously messy, so the tactile feelings of having your hands totally saturated in it are somewhat overwhelming. I kept a sink full of warm water and a step stool nearby because they wanted to wash their hands often but also wanted to get right back to work. The children created animal shapes, volcanoes, ocean waves, abstract designs of peaks and craters, a beach, meatballs, snails, and a melted Hershey's® chocolate kiss. The plaster proved to be a satisfying art activity inspired by original thoughts.

Chapter 7

Painting and Experimenting with Color

■

Paint, Paint Supplies, and Patience

Giving children a variety of art experiences promotes motor control, offers emotional satisfaction, enjoyment, and stimulates creative ideas. Young children are considered "born painters." A paintbrush in the hand of a child allows for natural, poised, and rhythmic movements. Children feel relaxed and free to paint with their minds and bodies and souls (D'Amico, 1953).

Painting gives children power and freedom. Painting gives satisfaction for emotional release (the freedom) and the power to change and re-create an idea within one's work of art. Painting is stimulating. Children can express their ideas, expand on them, and generate new ideas.

You will have to be the judge of when to introduce the very young children to painting activities based on how much interest they show in painting, how much they understand, and how developmentally appropriate you can make the activity.

Besides understanding the importance of providing young children with developmentally appropriate painting experiences the only other supplies you need include:

Paper: plain white, construction paper, computer paper, or grocery bags cut to lie flat.

Paints: Large bottles of water paints last a very long time. At first buy only red, yellow, blue, and white paint to let the children experiment creating their own spectrum of color.

Paintbrushes: have an assortment of differing sizes available to facilitate various forms of art expression.

Paint holders: (Use your imagination!)

We have used the plastic lids from any container. Save enough for each child to have a set for each paint color (and one for water to rinse their brushes).

I have collected large uncracked seashells—they make excellent individual paint pots!

Save the Styrofoam trays meats are wrapped in from your grocery store. Save enough trays for each child to have their own. Pour a color in each corner of the tray. Individual sets of paint holders are important because each child approaches paint differently. Some children dab their paintbrush in every color and then paint! Other children enjoy painting with one color at a time to be blended on their paper—not in their paint holder.

Ecologically speaking, reusing these unrecyclable Styrofoam trays counteracts their adverse effects.

Paint smocks: Large T-shirts donated from parents or older brothers and sisters of the children work beautifully. The larger size on small children protects their clothing.

Patience: Your patience and understanding is an important art supply integral to developing the values of art.

The children have to feel your approval of their actions. They need your recognition and enjoy your encouragement. Remember your two and three year olds are still in the scribbling stage. Older threes may begin creating recognizable forms and images. Fours and fives create images representative of their thinking. Have patience with each child at each developmental stage. Creative thoughts and actions are discouraged by comparing children's artwork or criticizing children's artwork in adult terms (adult reality).

Your perceptive criticism should recognize the special styles and qualities of each child's artwork. According to Howard Gardner (as cited in Brandt, 1987/1988), your perceptive criticism in art helps children "learn to see better, to hear better, to make finer discriminations and to see connections between things."

■

Experimental Activities with Color

Children respond quickly and enthusiastically to color. They enjoy color. Color in their artwork may symbolically represent concepts of people, objects, events, and experiences children try to convey through paint. They play with the colors of their paints to express feelings and ideas. Yellow may represent sunlight, red may be fire, a blur of blue may symbolically represent a summertime sky, water, or whatever children can imagine.

Children learn by doing; so what better way to learn colors than by creating them yourself? Since color is experimental for children, you only need red, blue, yellow, and white for them to start mixing.

Changing Colors

You will need: water, an empty egg carton, red, blue, yellow, and white paints or food coloring, and questions (guessing the colors).

What to do:

- Fill an empty egg carton half way with water.

- Squirt a few drops of paint (or food coloring) in each section. For example, prepare three red sections, three blue, three yellow, three white.

- Squirt a different color into each section.

- Observe the changes.

Color Racing

You will need: paper towels, colored markers, a plate of water, and cheerleading enthusiasm.

What to do:

- Ask the children, "Is it possible for colors to race?" Answer: "Let's figure it out!"

- Cut up a paper towel or napkin into single-layered squares.

- Draw a FINISH LINE across the paper towel two inches up from the bottom.

- Provide four to six different colored markers for the children to share.

- Ask the children to color in the bottom section of the paper towel below the FINISH LINE with different colors.

- Dip *only* the *edge* of the towel into the plate of water.

- As the towel starts absorbing the color, cheer for your favorite color to cross the FINISH LINE first! (Purple always seems to win.)

Color with Ice Cubes

You will need: an ice cube tray, food coloring, crayons or paints, paper, drinking glasses, and warm water or warm hands.

What to do:

- Fill an ice cube tray with water.

- Use food coloring to prepare four red cubes, four blue cubes, four yellow cubes.

- Allow to freeze.

- When ice cubes are frozen, give each child a piece of paper and red, blue, and yellow crayons or paints.

- Ask one child at a time to select one colored ice cube and put it in a small clear glass. Then have all the children put that color on their paper.

- Ask another child to select a different colored ice cube to add to the glass. Now add this color to the paper with the crayons or paint.

- As the ice cubes melt together a new color is made.

- Have the children pass the glass around. Handling the glass helps melt the ice cubes.

- Or, you can add a few drops of hot water or warm the glass first to speed the melting process.

- Let the children see and compare for themselves the colors mixed on their paper with the colors mixed in the glass.

Crayon Melt Designs

You will need: paper and wax paper, a warm iron, a potato peeler, crayons, and an imagination.

Gather the children to discuss the supplies and required safety measures concerning the potato peeler and iron.

What to do:

- Give each child a piece of paper and a piece of wax paper.

- Let each child pick out five or six different colored crayons.

- Your job is to peel the paper off of the crayons selected and with the potato peeler shave a few pieces of each crayon onto the paper.

- Place the wax paper over the paper and press with the warm iron.

- Let the paper cool a few seconds and have the child open their design. This is one of the all-time favorite color experiments. It stimulates the imagination, aids language development, and creates very interesting color blends and designs!

Making Rainbow Crayons

You will need: crayons, a potato peeler, cupcake tin, foil baking cups (to line the cupcake tin), preheated oven @ 400°, and children eager to color with homemade crayons.

What to do:

- Preheat oven to 400°.

- Line cupcake tin with foil baking cups.

- Collect very small broken pieces of different colored crayons or peel different colors with the potato peeler into baking cups.

- After three to five minutes children will see the wax melt into a liquid form.

- Remove and allow to cool and harden.

- Color!

Marble Painting

You will need: paint smocks (T-shirts),
four marbles, four colors of paint,
four paint holders, cardboard gift box
or shoe box, paper, and enthusiasm.

What to do:

- Line the box with a piece of paper.

- Put a few drops of each paint into the paint holders (plastic lids, shells, plastic dishes).

- Let each child drop a marble into each paint holder.

- Coat the marble with paint and then have the children drop the marbles onto the paper inside the box.

- Wiggle and shake the box for the marbles to crash, bang, and bounce into each other!

Magic Shaving Cream

You will need: paint smocks, can of white shaving cream, zip-loc® bags
for each child, red, blue, and yellow paints, and curiosity aroused by
these supplies.

What to do:

- Squirt some shaving cream into each child's zip-loc® bag.

- Ask each child to select two colors of paint.

- Drip one color of paint into the bag, seal the bag, and let the child squeeze the color into the shaving cream.

- Add another selected color, seal the bag, and squeeze.

- See the brand new mushed together color!

Upon seeing the new color in the bag, Joshua yelled out, "Magic!" Everyone enjoyed mushing their colors together.

Since it was during the Halloween and Thanksgiving season, I gave each child a piece of paper cut in a pumpkin shape titled, "The Magic Pumpkin." Not quite 4 year old Jenny had her zip-loc® bag filled with deep orange-sienna colored shaving cream. Jenny wanted to paint her paper pumpkin. She talked about the two colors she had chosen to squirt into her bag. I then gave each child red and yellow paint in their paint holders and they painted their "Magic Pumpkins" too! They plowed right into work harvesting "magic" orange paper pumpkins.

Not every art activity has to be a project or an experiment. Young children are much more interested in their artwork as they are working. Let children paint regularly for the sake of expressing themselves. I provide color experiments for children to see new relationships between previously unrelated objects or ideas. Such art experiences offer children a chance to invent new ideas and see innovative ways of relating objects familiar (or not familiar) to them within their environment. Color experiments stimulate divergent thinking. Painting experiences stimulate originality. The consistency of our care offers children the continuity required to master the feel and the confidence of their own personal skills in artistic expression.

Other art activities and creative experiences might include:

Swirl O' Paint or Spin Art: manufactured by Ohio Art, nasta toy co., NSI (Natural Science) in toy or craft stores for approximately $9.99. Paint is dripped onto a piece of paper spinning upon a motorized tray.

Splatter Paint: paint flicked off the end of paintbrushes or toothbrushes. (large paper and smocks recommended)

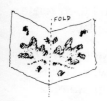

Butterfly Painting: fold paper in half, paint on one side of the fold, fold paper over painted side then press with the hands or roll with rolling pin.

Finger Painting: dipping their fingers into the paint provides a sheer sensory experience.

Mural Painting: Last spring I taped ten feet of paper on an outdoor fence. My actions were met with enthusiasm by the children. Mural painting meets the needs of every age—the theme can be a simple or complex process, depending on each child's capacity. The spaciousness of the paper lets children make the large, bold movements common in young children and mural paintings. Mural painting encourages freedom and usually serves to answer a social value. The four 4 year olds in this group sectioned off the paper with bold lines and agreed among themselves to stay within their own section. Democracy is the social value here. The length of each section did allow for the freedom of movement and the freedom of their imaginative thoughts to be expressed in broad, bold concepts. The characteristics of children's artwork tend to have the same aesthetic values of mural painting: very primitive, simple, and direct.

There is very little "work" involved for you while children are painting. You have very little control over childrens' designs. Your "work" involves enriching the painting experience for each child through encouraging questions and suggestions and by making the whole environment stimulating. Recognize the child's ability to paint and affirm that ability at every developmental stage.

■

Extending Color Concepts Through Stories

Reading a story to extend color concepts might be just the right type of "work" to do to stimulate your environment. Reading stories generates many new ideas. Children learn to think, talk, and then relate the story and characters to their own play.

❑ **IF** you read a story, such as *Mr. Rabbit and the Lovely Present,* by Charlotte Zolotow, and illustrated by Maurice Sendak, the children are given beautiful images of objects and colors. A little girl asks Mr. Rabbit to help her gather a birthday present for her mother. Through a beautifully illustrated stroll they talk about the color of various objects, share colorful ideas, and gather fruits: red apples, green pears, yellow bananas, and blue grapes, to arrange a birthday fruit basket. Mr. Rabbit talks about specific types of birds and the colors of precious gems. But, some of the objects may not be familiar objects to young children.

❑ **THEN** your "work" would involve extending these colors even further to relate to concepts and objects the children in your group would like to talk about.

❑ **HOW?** Children learn by doing. They will use their imaginations. Read the same story at another time and talk about the blue sapphires and green emeralds Mr. Rabbit suggests the little girl might give her mother for the birthday gift. Sapphires? Emeralds? I have accumulated a bucket of collected and donated costume jewelry the children use for pretend, dress-up play. We dumped the entire bucket out and looked for precious gems. Not only did we discover blue sapphires and green emeralds but crystals and diamonds and red rubies! This discovery was surely a treasure. The children asked if they could paint a treasure. We drew big rectangular treasure chests on large pieces of paper. The children had blue, yellow, red, and white paints and mixed and blended the colors to make sacks of gold, chains of emeralds, caches of diamonds and royal sapphires.

There are over 40,000 children's books to choose from. This is a very small list of books that are related to colors from *Read to Me! Teach Me!* (1982) by Mary Jane Mangini Rossi. Use this list as a quick reference to select books that may coincide with your art activities.

Bruna, Dick. *My Shirt is White*
Carle, Eric. *My Very First Book of Colors*
Chermayeff, Ivan. *Tomato and Other Colors*
Emberley, Ed. *Green Says Go*
Freeman, Don. *The Chalk Box Story*
Hirsch, Marilyn. *How the World Got It's Color*
Hoban, Tana. *Is It Red? Is It Yellow? Is It Blue?*
Lionni, Leo. *Little Blue and Little Yellow; A Color of His Own*
Peek, Merle. *Mary Wore a Red Dress*
Reiss, John. *Colors*
Rossetti, Christina. *What Is Pink?*
Slobodkina, Esphyra. *Caps for Sale*
Tison, Annette, and Talus Taylor. *Adventures of the Three Colors*
Zolotow, Charlotte. *Mr. Rabbit and the Lovely Present*

❑ **IF** you value a stimulating environment for children to think, learn, and do their work/play in;

❑ **THEN** you must discover ways to encourage young children to think about their whole environment. Learn about the people and objects in their environment and do related activities that promote sensitive relationships within that environment.

Chapter 8

Creative Play Using Three-Dimensional Materials

■

Arranging a Housekeeping Center

Did you ever wonder why every nursery school and kindergarten class has a housekeeping center? The housekeeping area connects the familiar, direct, sensitive relationship between a child's own home and their day care environment. Children transfer the people and events in their own home life into play situations that have happened, they pretend could happen, or wish would happen.

In the eyes of children, their greatest joy in terms of time, space, innovative opportunities, and initiative is working on and in three-dimensional materials: block building, sculpture molding, and discarded cardboard appliance boxes.

❑ **IF** you want to arrange a housekeeping center;

❑ **THEN** fortunately you have many options, ranging from simple constructions to enterprising feats to expensive investments (such as toy sinks and stoves that can cost $59 to $99 on sale).

❑ **HOW?** To construct simple housekeeping areas:

Design one area of a room with a table and chairs and a box of toy plates, cups, saucers, utensils, pots and pans, or plastic cups, bowls, and spoons, aluminum pie plates and coffee pots. Lend pot holders, kitchen towels, any kitchen gadget such as an egg beater, egg slicer, potato masher, or egg timer.

Save large discarded boxes from supermarkets or appliance stores. Transform these treasures into sinks and stoves with junk materials and paints. Remove metal strippings and staples from boxes *before* children play with them to avoid any safety hazards.

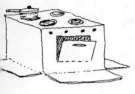

Stopping in your travels to save a discarded appliance box is an enterprising feat. It is worth *every* ounce of effort. I have even asked friends and neighbors with station wagons or trucks to help me gather discarded boxes I have spotted in local areas.

One afternoon while in an appliance store I asked a salesperson what happens to all of the boxes once the appliances are delivered. I was told they get folded up and put next to the dumpster on the side of the building. I thought to myself how much easier it would be to transport the boxes "folded up"! And then the salesperson added, "Come by before noon, that's when the dumpster is collected." Unfortunately the store didn't make an appliance sale that day but has become a good resource center.

Another available resource is a paint or hardware store that sells wallpaper. Go in and ask for any discontinued wallpaper books.

The most convenient situation, however, is to ask your neighbors to donate empty washer, dryer, or refrigerator boxes. Transforming discarded or donated boxes has become a major creative activity of my program. The children can enjoy this activity indoors or outdoors.

The refrigerator size box is the all-time favorite to convert into a house with paint and wallpaper. The children gather markers, paints, paste, scissors, and the wallpaper books. I slit doors and windows that flap open and closed and the children do the rest!

Just this past March we received a refrigerator size 'house' from an attentive, generous neighbor just before lunch. Unanimously, the children voted to eat lunch first (a little earlier than usual) and then decorate the box. As I was preparing lunch it started to snow. Seeing such forlorn faces I knew I had to react. We dressed warmly and went outside to "save the box." We managed to dismantle the box and drag it to the basement, reassemble it, and the group ate lunch in the box lying on its side. After lunch they painted and wallpapered the inside and outside of the box to protect it from the snow. They rearranged their kitchen play area inside the box and played "Mother and Father."

■

Creative Expression Through Housekeeping

The housekeeping experience has been the most successful in terms of including self-discovery and creative expression, along with social values and aesthetic awareness. What is so satisfying is to see the excitement and eagerness on every child's face—at every age! There is work and play involved for every child creating the "house." Every child enthusiastically tries on the role of "house" painter, interior decorator, carpenter, and gardener. It's fun to observe a two year old painting "flowers" all around the bottom of the box! The children assume roles of mothers, fathers, sisters, brothers, grandparents, babies, and even pets living in their house. Some pretend to deliver the mail to the house when given assorted envelopes to address, mail, and deliver. One 4 year old boy drew water meters on the outside of the "house" and came to read the family's water meter. And then he even handed them a bill! They paint pictures on the inside walls, curtains on the 'windows,' bricks on the outside walls, even a roof and a chimney! Weather permitting, this activity can literally last for days.

Children learn about themselves and real-life situations through play. The addition of three-dimensional materials offers activities that are used virtually every day throughout the year by children of every age.

PART THREE

Music and Creative Listening

Chapter 9

Appreciating Music

■

Finding the Right Music

A voluminous amount of appropriate songs and rhymes does exist specifically for young children to enjoy and parents and caregivers to appreciate. But there is so much music! We would be slighting the tremendous power of music if we concentrated on finding only children's songs in our work and care of children.

Children's songs and nursery rhymes are wonderful to use for happy musical activities, fun little finger plays, and as helpful teaching tools to pass on our favorite traditional melodies. However, eight years ago when my son Joseph was an infant, I found myself seriously and quite carefully editing many *Mother Goose Nursery Rhymes*. Never before had I realized that several of these contained harsh, violent, and discriminatory language. This trend is eliminated in the book *Father Gander Nursery Rhymes* (as opposed to Mother Goose) by Father Gander (Douglas Larche).

This book is a compilation of many Mother Goose Nursery Rhymes heavily edited to reflect positive, respectful attitudes, healthy outlooks, and the value messages children need to hear. According to Father Gander (Douglas Larche), "For today's children it is time to take the delights of Mother Goose and apply them to the ideals we all want children to have— equality, love, responsibility, an appreciation of life and all living things, good nutrition and conservation of resources. Mother Goose has survived because of its musical and poetical merit, not its message. Why not take the best of the old and meld it with the positive message of work, love and ethics?"

Categories of Music

On my weekly treks to the library (with or without children) I select books by theme or child initiated interest and am now in the habit of doing the same for music by scouting out albums, audio cassettes, and compact discs (CDs). The categories of music to enjoy are quite extensive:

Bluegrass: a recorded anthology of American music.

Jazz: rhythm is the business of jazz.

Motion Pictures: 150 years of original motion picture soundtracks.

Musical shows: albums of show tunes are good choices—the jacket cover explains the story and characters, and with this musical information children can act the story out.

Rock: has defended or tried to justify and explain social/cultural temperature and its elemental environment.

Orchestral: for children, orchestral music gives free reign to a child's imagination.

Classical: keyboard, strings, wind, or vocal classical music is capable of producing a great range of feelings.

Folk Music: traditional ethnic music played on an enormous variety of fascinating instruments.

Country and Western: cowboy songs awash in country music.

Electronic Music: sounds produced by electronic and computer-driven instruments.

Humor: recorded comedy routines with or without music.

International Popular Music: songs you know by heart (often without even realizing it) due to a catchy

unforgettable phrase, its good tune, a certain senti-
ment, or the personality of the performer(s).

Rhythm and Blues: raw, personal, and powerful.

Operas and Operetta: a tragic, funny, heroic, or
mysterious story entirely set to music that opera
singers must sing as well as act out.

Ballet: principle dancers and/or an entire troupe
dance to music to express the action and meaning of
a story.

Religious Music: started as an outgrowth of plain-
song/folksong—a simple chant sung in church.

The Current Popular category includes:

Popular Songs	Musicals
Marches	Ragtime
Jazz	Swing
Blues	Rhythm and Blues
Rock Music	Reggae
Progressive Rock	Punk Rock
Soul—Gospel	Folk
Folk/Rock	Boogie Woogie

By recording the music you select onto audio-cas-
settes you'd be surprised how quickly an interesting,
diverse, personal collection of music you can establish. Doing so has become a lesson in music appreciation for me as well as the children.

■

Exploring Other Cultures Through Music

Young children should be introduced to the music,
values, and traditions of other cultures along with
their own. They have an uncanny ability to collect
and absorb so much mental data and then process
such information so fruitfully. Children create knowledge out of the ordinary on a daily basis. Presenting

different cultural costumes, dress, values, and traditions to young children in a stimulating fashion through their play enhances their ever widening spectrum of dance and song.

Informative writer and musician Neil Ardley (1986) explains, "Music is something that people everywhere seem to need to enhance their lives. Music has tremendous power to affect human feelings, especially when used to accompany words and movement in singing and dancing. It can raise or lower the spirits, help people work or relax, intensify religious experience and confer importance on ceremonies and occasions. Throughout the world, people have developed many distinctive ways of making music."

The range of music produced throughout the world is as fascinating as the range of its people. Classical music arose and developed over the past 400 years in Europe, North America, and Russia. Ever since, its permeating effect has been influencing musicians throughout the world. When the rhythmic drive of Africa was transported to North America, it merged with European styles of music to create jazz, rock, soul, and country music.

In America with its own range of people from throughout the world, the children in our care need to begin to develop multi-cultural considerations.

We tend to think that surely all children must play and act, need and want, scream, cry, and sing the same. But music is so heavily seeped within a culture that it can, and should, preserve a pride and could even identify a culture. Children are emersed in their cultures also. Children may play and act similarly globally but through music young children can learn how to listen, sing, and dance to the music of their own culture while enjoying the music of others.

The basic curriculum of any early childhood setting should be accepting and developing each and every child as a unique individual both because of and apart from their culture. Young children should be given opportunities and experiences to see and interact with one another as individuals, rather than on a basis of ethnic, cultural, or racial differences.

❏ **IF** the appreciation and respect of inter-group similarities and differences is essential;

❏ **THEN** we need to bear in mind and follow through with the understanding that if we help children determine the larger scope of their commonalities: that they all need shelter, food, and clothing, then smaller cultural differences could be better understood and appreciated by them.

❏ **HOW?** Choose the music of different cultures. Introducing young children to the music and songs of many different cultural backgrounds transmits the knowledge that people are more alike than they are different in many parts of the world. Parents and caregivers can aim at exploring similarities that cross cultures with children and then branch out and discover cultural diversities.

Handbooks and songbooks with multi-cultural information, activities, and resources provide avenues of awareness and an exploration of ideas based on these macro-cultural similarities. Read stories from and about other countries to stimulate discussions and brainstorming exercises. Such experiences might involve the artwork, tools, storytelling, and games with different origins. But the music from other parts of the world relays the concept we need to help children understand, that the needs of people in various places and situations are basically the same. Music can travel across cultures to convey nuances, create subtleties, and bind children.

❏ **WHY?** Music contributes to our sense of identity and esteem. Parents and caregivers can help children keep a sense of pride in their own ethnic heritage, even if they are in the process of learning about a new one.

■

Using Music to Develop Listening Skills

The musical activities that have worked for me have developed over time. Musical activities occur spontaneously. Creative movement set to music could happen on any day with a child's request, through their play, or through my asking. Toddlers and preschool age children need to feel their bodies in motion. Children need your help to develop listening skills so they can learn to appreciate and respond to music.

Organizing and planning an activity with the children facilitates listening skills. Describe whatever activity you may have in mind, and explain ideas, procedures, expectations, and offer reasons for doing the activity. Brainstorm with the children and ask for their ideas and suggestions. One idea leads to another. Everyone is listening and learning from each other. Developing listening skills is essential for all children. That feeling of participating in a group applies to every aspect of a child's life—within their family, among their peers—in any social situation children need to feel that others are listening to them so they in turn can learn to listen to others.

Chapter 10

Active Learning Through Music

■

The Importance of Music

Music is everywhere. Children hear music in their homes if and when family members are listening to the radio, to records, or tapes. Children hear music on the car radio while being transported from place to place by families meeting the demands of the busy schedules they keep. Children hear music on TV. They recognize theme songs of favorite cartoons or shows. Children also hear music on the street. But this is not the same as listening to and appreciating music.

❏ **IF** it is important to encourage young children to listen to and appreciate music;

❏ **THEN** children need our help to learn how to respond to music.

❏ **HOW?** With any game or activity set to any type of music or song.

❏ **WHY?** During the course of a day a child's feelings may range from joyous, to aggressive, to hungry, to wanting to be alone, to feeling left alone. During one activity a child may be very cooperative yet other times the same child may feel rebellious. Music helps unleash all of the feelings that emerge or well up within a child.

Music helps develop listening techniques.

Music helps children learn to move their bodies in time and space.

Music activities introduce young children to various types of music and musical instruments.

Music can be relaxing.

Music can be interpreted.

Music stimulates the mind *and* body.

Music activities offer children a chance to share ideas, to participate, and to be members of a group.

Music lets children express individual feelings.

■

Musical Activities

Nursery rhymes and traditional melodies are great to use as an early introduction to music. You can sing nursery rhymes, play musical instruments, and hear and learn the words of a rhyme or song.

❑ **IF** children learn through their senses—seeing, hearing, smelling, tasting, and touching;

❑ **THEN** the more senses used during one activity the more impact and valuable you can make the musical experience.

❑ **HOW?** Start with a basic traditional melody— Humpty Dumpty.

How many children even realize Humpty Dumpty is (was) an egg?

When you are ready to begin this activity, gather a few props together for effect if you can:

an egg; 1 or 2 toy horses; 1 or 2 toy people.

Now gather the children. Talk about learning new songs. Ask if anyone knows the Humpty Dumpty song, then begin by singing the song. Anyone who knows the song will chime in also.

Your first objective has been accomplished: everyone is listening. Children learn songs basically through listening and repeating. But that's too passive. The children need to actively learn.

If possible find an illustrated nursery rhyme book and show the group the picture of Humpty Dumpty sitting on the wall. If you don't have such a book draw a simple sketch of an egg sitting on a wall; or hold a real egg on top of a wooden block or bench. Read the song like a story. Ask the children if they would like to be any of the characters in the story. Read it again as they act the song out with the horses and people (king's men).

Talk about the song. Ask questions: "What is going to happen if this egg falls off of this wall?" or "Can the king's men help Humpty Dumpty if he falls off?"

Sing the song again and see your results. Think of the impact you have just made on your group. You are able to formulate and weave the gist of the song into a meaningful context. The children are able to hear the tune, listen to the words, sing the song, feel like the characters of the rhyme, and use their minds and bodies to act the story out! (Really let the egg fall off the wall onto a dish and have scrambled eggs for lunch!) Children learn by using their senses. They don't need a lot of props and gimmicks to learn.

❏ **WHY?** Children like activities to flow simply and smoothly. Too much material is distracting to children and they get lost in the clutter. If the group loses interest you may lose your patience and any valuable, teachable moments get lost in the confusion. Plan and organize your ideas. It is important to remember that your ideas should stem from the children's play to keep their interest alive. While children are playing and forming concepts about the situations they are actively involved in, your ideas should be an extension of their play. Any song can be done similarly. Just remember to involve the children's ideas for the most effective active learning to take place.

The Piano "Lesson"

❏ **IF** you want to disprove theorists' claims that young children have short attention spans;

❏ **THEN** create interesting, developmentally appropriate activities for them.

❏ **HOW?** One morning I heard two year old Matthew trying to make heads or tails out of Rain, Rain Go Away combined with Mary's lamb going to school. I asked two girls, Kate and Amanda (both three year olds), if they recognized the song Matt was trying to sing. The girls led Matt to the piano where a songbook was located. I followed. My intention was not to play the songs on the piano and have them sit and listen, but for Matthew to learn the two songs separately with our help. Matt, Kate, and Amanda sat on the piano bench ready to play. I sat to the side of the piano to listen, read the words, and sing along. Kate and Amanda knew the words and took full charge. They "played" the piano and sang each song out loud. After a few "lessons" I asked them to let Matt have a chance to "play" the piano (as they did) and repeat their words. They all "played" and sang together for 45 minutes! They turned each page of *The Golden Songbook* and "played" every song as if reading the music!

Not only did Matthew enjoy learning two songs but this activity also provided an important precursor to reading—understanding that written words hold meaning. Pretending to "read" music, playing together, "reading," scribbling and reading stories aloud are all important preliminary methods of child's play that develop language, the skills for writing, and the joy of reading.

❏ **WHY?** At this early age, children should not be expected to engage in creative learning activities merely to produce a product; but rather to be allowed to express themselves and enjoy the process.

If I had sat down to play the songs correctly for them their enthusiasm would have been lost. I would have been setting an example—by knowing the notes—that they would assume I wanted them to follow. I had no intention of teaching them how to play the songs on the piano (not yet, anyway). My only intention was to help Matt learn the words to the songs. Kate and Amanda thoroughly enjoyed their roles as music teachers to Matthew. To appreciate music children have to appreciate their own involvement with music.

■

"Families" of Musical Instruments

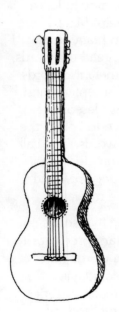

Playing with a musical instrument gives the children an idea of what you're suppose to *do* with the instrument. An illustrated book of instruments offers children the opportunity to see and discuss the graduated size of the related instruments, compare the number of holes, count the number of keys, or imagine the sound each could produce. Guitars, for instance, are to pluck and strum. And though to a child a guitar may look similar to the violin, the instruments in the violin family require a bow.

The violin family is comprised of:

1. the violin
2. the viola
3. the cello
4. the double bass

And unless you have an illustration to compare and discuss the graduated size difference of each instrument, they may all appear basically the same.

Next consider all of the woodwind instruments of an orchestra:

1. The simple whistle
2. The recorder family
   a. soprano recorder
   b. treble recorder
   c. tenor recorder
   d. bass recorder

3. The flute family:
   a. bass flute
   b. alto flute
   c. piccolo

All of the woodwind instruments are basically pipes. As air is blown into the pipe the air vibrates and then is released as a note through the open holes. The greater the length of vibrating air, the deeper the sound. The holes of the larger woodwind instruments are covered by pads and are operated by keys. This system of keys allows a musician to produce more than forty notes by opening and closing the holes simultaneously!

The reed instruments contain one or two thin stiff reeds that vibrate and produce sound when blowing air across the mouthpiece:

1. oboes
2. bassoons
3. clarinets

The clarinet family includes:

1. bass clarinet
2. basset horn
3. soprano clarinet
4. sopranino clarinet

These woodwind reed instruments have ancient or early origins. A fairly new addition to the reed family is the saxophone. The saxophone was invented in 1840 by combining the mouthpiece of the clarinet

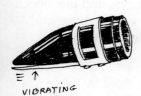

≡ ↑
VIBRATING
REED

with a system of keys and the conical pipe of the oboe. The varying sizes in the saxophone family produce the sound of the:

1. soprano saxophone
2. alto saxophone
3. tenor saxophone
4. baritone saxophone

And now consider the majestic and stirring sounds of the brass family: the trumpets, trombones, tubas, and the French horn. There is nothing quite like a brass band in a parade or at a country fair to exhilarate its listeners with its lively, driving, marching beat!

The percussion instruments give music life. This family of instruments includes the: maracas, castanets, woodblocks, triangles, cymbals, gongs, xylophones, and drums. The beat of the drum propels the music which then becomes emphasized by accompanying musicians. Whether listening to folk music, rock, jazz, or pop, the drums effects produce that basic beat we feel that makes us want to dance or move.

■

The Focused Field Trip

❏ **IF** you want to put all of these categorized instruments into the minds and hands of children;

❏ **THEN** plan a focused field trip.

❏ **HOW?** In the center of your town or city (or at your nearest mall) find a music store. After a music activity involving instruments focus on one specific instrument. Read stories, find pictures, and talk about the size of the instrument, its shape, and the sound the instrument produces. Then plan a trip to the music store to discover first hand.

❏ **WHY?** The purpose of a music store field trip allows children to focus on one particular family of instruments. (Having read the list of musical instrument families, it's quite extensive and simply overwhelming for a child.) A trip with a specific purpose helps children "see" and understand with their minds:bodies in motion. This promotes active learning.

In my town we have a store called The Guitar Experience. I took a group of six 3 and 4 year old children to visit this shop. The people that work there where a bit surprised at a group of such young clientele, but they were quite enthusiastic and attentive. The children asked them a lot of questions and the salespeople answered by pointing out the similarities and the differences between the acoustic and electric guitars. They even took the time to relate experiences they had had with different styles of guitars.

They showed us how to hold a guitar and let the children pluck and strum a few different types—especially the fuschia colored electric guitar and the one with the black and white checkerboard design! We browsed through the rack of sheet music and songbooks for guitars and looked at the whole array of colorful guitar straps.

Through another focused field trip we have discovered The Drum Studio. The store manager and owner allowed the children to play the xylophone with different types of padded wooden hammers. He let them feel the weight of different drumsticks and mallets. He tapped the cymbals with each to show the children their different effects. He let them "play" the cymbals with the wire brushes which produced a very pleasant though sophisticated sound. When they pressed the foot pedal of the bass drum they looked surprised that they could produce such a big booming sound.

A young boy around nine years old came into the studio for a drum lesson. While he waited for his instructor, I asked if he would play something on the drums for us. He seemed a little timid yet simultaneously eager to impress this group of youngsters. He obliged. It was fun to see a young child himself showing even younger children his joy in playing an instrument. We clapped and thanked him and the owner when the boy was through. We left the store when the instructor arrived so we wouldn't interfere with his lesson.

Plan a focused field trip. Look in your local telephone book or around your neighborhood to find music stores near you.

Once children have seen and experienced the real thing, a stimulated imagination can work to create or invent a new instrument or re-create the instruments of a field trip using common household products.

■

Homemade Musical Instruments

Music can be appreciated through singing, repeating, listening, and dancing. The mind and body become involved. Having musical instruments adds one more dimension to any music activity. It doesn't have to be a major expense. I have picked up an old guitar at a garage sale for only 50¢. Ask friends and neighbors if they have instruments you can borrow for a short time to introduce the children to different types of musical instruments and the sounds they produce. Or you can even have the children make their own instruments: guitars, xylophones, and drums. Here are the steps to take to do these activities:

Guitars

Another way to make a guitar involves using a cigar box. I asked the owner of a local deli if he would be kind enough to save empty cigar boxes for me. I explained that my work involved caring for young children and I wanted to use cigar boxes for an activity. I left my name on a bag in his store and frequented the store for coffee and lottery tickets on weekends to stay friendly and visible. After a few weeks he gave me the bag with eight empty cigar boxes.

At that time my group consisted of two 3 year olds, two 4 year olds, one 5 year old, and a toddler. We all participated in a musical activity: the toddler played that 50¢ guitar while the older children playfully danced for her. Listening and singing and dancing along with the group was appropriate for the toddler, making the guitar was not. While the other children made their guitars, I gave the toddler one of the cigar boxes and a spoon and she busily played alongside producing more "music."

Cigar Box Guitars

You will need: one cigar box, 6 assorted size elastic bands, 2 pieces of cardboard 3" long x 2" wide, tape, and 12 tacks.

What to do:

1. Punch out 6 holes in the lids of the cigar box (see illustration).

2. Glue or tape the lid shut.

3. Have the children cut the rubber bands in half and arrange from the thickest to the thinnest.

4. Tack the rubber bands down across the top of the lid.

5. Draw 3 lines half an inch apart on the cardboard pieces.

6. Fold along each line to make a triangular shape. Tape to hold shape.

7. Have the children slide the 2 cardboard triangles under the rubber bands near the edge of the lid.

8. Play the guitar! Listen to the difference between the vibrations of the thin rubber bands and the thicker ones.

9. Move the triangular shapes around under the rubber bands. This changes the sound because you increase or decrease the vibrations.

10. Have the children experiment on their own.

Source: M. L. Keen, *The How and Why Book of Science Experiments* (Los Angeles: Price/ Stern, Sloan, 1985). Used with permission.

For $1.49 you can purchase Martin Keen's *The How and Why Wonder Book of Science Experiments* (1985) which shows how to make a guitar and explains the way they work.

As a related learning experience, I have taken the front panel of the piano off to have each child pluck the strings inside. They see the graduated thickness of each string and hear the difference between the fat and skinny strings when the keys are pressed.

A toy xylophone is a good example to use when explaining about different sizes and lengths producing different sounds. The children can see the varying lengths of each bar on the xylophone and hear the difference between the longest and shortest bars. Of course you can have the children make their own xylophone.

Xylophones

You will need: 8 drinking glasses all the same size, placed in a row, and a spoon.

What to do:

1. Have the children count out 8 glasses and line them up.

2. Pour 1/2 inch of water in the first glass and let the children take turns adding a little more water to each succeeding glass.

3. Have the children tap gently on the rim of each glass with the spoon. The amount of air left in each glass changes the sound produced.

Drums

You will need: oatmeal containers, plastic containers with their lids, or cookie tins with their lids.

What to do:

• Let the children experiment with cotton swabs, bottle brushes, paintbrushes, or pegs to create their own drumsticks.

• Let the children go through a junk drawer to discover their own interesting ways to make drumsticks. Supervise for safety reasons.

• Form a percussion section and play away!

• Don't forget the original homemade drum set—pots, pans, and wooden spoons! Pot lids and aluminum pie plates make a great set of cymbals for a complete percussion section.

Appreciating Toy Musical Instruments

Yes, they are loud and noisy, but they are fun. Marching and banging and stamping and singing out loud are exciting responses children feel when expressing themselves with their music. Permitting children to do so shows you respect their form of creative musical expression.

You will have days, however, when you just can't cope with a high noise, high energy, musically creative group of children. You are the role model and you set the atmosphere of your home. If an activity won't work for you—it can't work for the children.

That feeling overcame me one morning when I saw 4 year old Jeff walk into the room with a toy drum draped around his neck. He brought it to me to open to get the drumsticks out. I had to think fast. I didn't want to tell him to put the drum away so I asked the other members of the group if they would like to dance while Jeff played the drum. I told them the living room rug was the stage, the floorlamp a spotlight, and I played a cassette tape of Dvorak's *New World Symphony*. The piece is slow, dramatic, spirited in certain measures but beautifully and completely peaceful.

On days when you feel out of sorts, let the music take over. Allow music to relax your inner being. You have developed your own taste in music out of your own preferences, influences, and culture. Enjoy them!

Jeff was still able to express himself with his music and Brianne, 2 years old; Kate, 3; Jessica, 5; Lauren, 5; and Joseph, 5, beautifully expressed themselves through dance. They created and organized an imaginary stage production set to music. Yes, the energy level was high but not loud and chaotic. Therefore I could appreciate their actions and the music.

Chapter 11

Creative Movement

■

Appreciating Movement Through Music

Musical experiences can range from simple to complex. Start with a simple activity. Gather the children around a radio. Turn on any station. Gather the children around a record player. Play any record. Ask questions and let the children talk about the music they hear. "Do you hear that drum beat?" or "Do you like the voice singing this song?" Offer information, "That's the sound of a saxophone, . . . a guitar, . . . a piano." Talk about instruments and sounds they are familiar with. Get your group into the habit of listening and responding to the music they hear and how it makes them feel.

❏ **IF** music is playing someone always starts dancing.

❏ **THEN** the others generally follow. If the children appreciate music, movement will follow.

❏ **HOW?** If children begin dancing to music you play, they are listening to the sounds they hear in their surroundings. It is important to recognize observant behavior and encourage and affirm listening skills. Children need you to reassure their actions to reinforce their confidence. If a child is reluctant to join in, don't force the issue. Let them sit and watch if they want to. Or you can suggest that they pretend to be part of an audience watching the musical show. You can quietly cut up pieces of paper and have the child pretend to sell tickets to the show.

❏ **WHY?** You are gradually enlarging the complexity of the "music show" concept and you are allowing the child to express himself/herself individually and still feel like a member of the group. Feeling good about yourself in social interactions and within social situations is an important developmental task we all must face.

■

Simple Activities Set to Music

❑ **IF** you tie a balloon on a string for each dancing child;

❑ **THEN** they move more creatively and rhythmically trying to follow the rhythm of the balloon.

❑ **IF** you give each child a kitchen towel, a woolen scarf, a silky scarf, or any piece of material to dance with, and let them use their prop in whatever way they imagine;

❑ **THEN** they may wave it behind them, wiggle it in front of themselves, or wrap it around themselves. I have even seen a boy tuck a scarf in his waistband and call it a tail. If allowed to think for themselves children expand on their own ideas, such as how it feels to have a tail like a dog or a cat. They can pretend to be horses, elephants, or even mice depending on the rhythm of the music they hear.

❑ **HOW?** It helps children to feel their bodies in motion. Children learn how to use their minds and bodies to: swing and sway; bend and stretch; rise and fall; twist and turn; shake and roll; and fall.

❑ **WHY?** By offering musical activities you are giving children a playful way to develop language through: the names of musical instruments, the names of songs, the words of the songs, each child describing their own actions and feelings through their movements. They become aware of contrasts in music: fast-slow, high-low, loud-soft. They are learning to participate within a group—individually and socially; emotionally and physically.

All of these factors enhance a child's self-worth. They feel competent learning and knowing what their bodies are capable of doing. The better you make children feel about themselves the more eager they are to cooperate and try new experiences and activities with you.

■

Musical Interpretations Through Dance

❏ **IF** I see a child flit, float, or rhythmically move across a room;

❏ **THEN** I recognize and acknowledge their dancing style. I encourage and affirm their listening response and relate and reassure their movements to the music.

❏ **HOW?** Through positive statements such as: "You really feel the beat of this song! That was a great kick!" "You really do look like a ballerina! That was a beautiful spin!" "That's exactly how a ballet dancer would leap!"

In a group we listen to measures of a musical piece and I ask questions about how the music makes them feel, what does the music sound like, and how does the music make them feel like moving. I jot down all of their responses *in consecutive order* to correspond to the music as we are listening to each particular composition. We listen to the piece again and I apply their responses symbolically to the music they were just listening to.

For example, we listened to one of the albums from our recorded library collection—The Cincinnati Pops Orchestra's version of Reznicek's "Donna Diana." As we listened I recorded their responses:

Kate (3 years, 5 months) says, "Sounds like they're jogging!"

Jenny (3 years, 2 months) says, "I'm riding my bike in the park."

As the music slowed young Mathew, (2 years, 6 months) says, "My bike has to get fixed now."

According to their interpretations, as the music gradually increased in volume, they announced, "all of their bikes have been fixed." At the loud crescendo Kate yelled, "Now my bike can fly!"

The entire group seems excited about the mental images being created. I play the piece again from the start, and again: the rug becomes a stage, the floor-lamp a spotlight! They remember the theme they have just created and act out their version of what they have just heard. They pretend to pedal bicycles, enter a bike race in the park, take their bikes to the repair shop, pedal again, and pretend to fly.

❏ **WHY?** Their feelings and movements have merged into the sounds of the music and a theatrical dance is beautifully conveyed. My encouragement and affirmation of their choreographic artistry provides incentive for other musical interpretations. Over time they have established quite a repertoire. Every composition or ballet d'action is outstanding and unique. I use the same format for each musical dance interpretation:

1. Play the record.

2. Ask questions.

3. Jot down their responses to the music as they are listening and reacting to what they hear.

4. Play the record again and let them dance. As they dance throw in cues now and then—"This is the part you said sounds like . . ." "You really look like you are . . ." (say their response) "This is the slow part you heard."

5. Applaud their efforts!

6. File their responses with the album or in the cassette or CD box.

Child Powered Musical Interpretations

Hap Palmer's children's song, "Slide Whistle Suite," is a child's study in movement. My current group of children ranging from 2 years, 4 months to 4 years old, have entitled it "Hunters that Protect the Hunted." The music of "Slide Whistle Suite" invites children to actively participate with creative movements. It is broken down into seven parts which consists of music to: 1. Walk; 2. Run; 3. Jump; 4. Skip; 5. Gallop; 6. Slide; 7. Walk.

As the children interpret these seven parts, they imagine they are on safari in the jungle and animals begin to follow them. They want to welcome the animals into their jungle campsite. A few of the children want to be the "good hunters," while the other children interpreted and visualized elephants stomping, gazelle running swiftly, bunnies hopping, frogs leaping, tigers and lions stretching, and birds swooping.

Corresponding to the sharp changes in the music, the "evil hunters" want to capture their new found animal friends. Consequently, the children are the good hunters that protect the hunted.

After hearing the song and initially listening to their eager responses, I began to collect details and props to elaborate their ideas and interpretations. The props were large pictures of animals cut from magazines. I glued these pictures onto pieces of cardboard and placed them all around the "jungle" room. They each wore a hat (any hat) to protect themselves from the burning jungle sun. They had a pair of toy binoculars, two telescopes to share, and toy guns. Each of the seven parts summons new animals into the campsite depending on how they interpret the music. They succeed in fending off the "evil hunters" and all of the animals come out of hiding. It's a masterpiece, an intellectual, artistic achievement on their part.

My group is currently "performing" Sergei Prokofiev's *Peter and the Wolf* (1934). This has been a long-running success! Even baby Hannah, our newest member, becomes a helping set designer. Hannah is not quite 2; but when she hears and recognizes the initial narration explaining the animals and characters being portrayed by the musical instruments, she gets "Peter" the rope he'll need and then helps lay the blocks as everyone builds "Grandfather's garden wall." The "stage crew" finishes the garden wall just in time to hear 4 year old Matt exclaim, "I'll be Leonard Bernstein!"

The Big Band Sound of Glenn Miller makes everyone of us want to dance and jump! The children didn't need to know the jitterbug to enjoy this music. To them, hearing "Tuxedo Junction" represented the personalities of three neighborhood cats. Their creative interpretation is playful, imaginative, and fun. The children dance, slink, kick, roll, slither, and jump around to the Big Band sound while pretending to be my neighbor's cats. They assume the boldness and confidence of one cat named Reebok; they pretend to be as shy and timid as Shadow; and then dance and act like Baby, the playful kitten.

It's important to note that not one of us was previously familiar with these musical selections. With creative thoughts, movements, and by encouraging their listening skills, the children are able to use their bodies and their minds to interpret the sounds they hear and the feelings they think the music represents. They invent creative works of art through music and dance.

Encourage the children to think about the music they hear. Have them "feel" the music through their interpretive movements. This gives them the opportunity to develop a coordination between their rhythmic movements, listening skills, and the mental images the music creates.

PART FOUR

Science

Chapter 12

Science: A Direct Approach

■

Active Learning Through Science

From birth children try to make sense of their world. Daily experiences with people, language, play, and activities increase their awareness of that world. Daily discoveries about themselves and their capabilities increase their involvement and interest in learning how to make relationships in their world.

Young children learn more about themselves and about their world when they investigate their immediate environment on their own. Children learn in an atmosphere that permits them to think, choose, and decide to do the work and play that meets their needs and interests them most. However, we can provoke this learning. We can share opportunities with children that help them see how things happen, let them make things happen, and understand why things happen. Exploring and investigating with science activities and experiments is a direct approach to learning.

One dictionary definition of science is, "the possession of knowledge of natural and physical phenomena." Isn't that what children do from the moment of birth? They begin to gather data about life through the growth and change of living things. They gather data about physical materials through their senses. They gather data about the physical laws of nature through activities that explore weight, motion and resistance; about the Earth through its temperatures and environments. All the while they are formulating a reserve of scientific knowledge. They are gathering a conceptual awareness of the world.

Methods of Inquiry

Let's explore some science ideas as I have shared them with the children. Scientists solve their problems when they:

1. Recognize a problem.

2. Collect information.

3. Invent a theory.

4. Do experiments.

5. Make conclusions.

Here is an example of how infants would solve a problem through the same method of inquiry:

1. They feel hungry (recognize a problem).

2. They think of past performances when feeling hungry (collect information).

3. They assume and test different cries (invent a theory).

4. They cry for attention (experiment).

5. They learn to communicate a need, learn to satisfy a need, learn to conclude through experimentation (make conclusions).

Here is an example of how pragmatic toddlers would solve a problem using the same method of inquiry:

1. They see blocks stacked like a tower (recognize a problem).

2. They think about how to get to the blocks. "Should I crawl or run?" They think about the builder of the tower (maybe) (collect information).

3. They assume and test different methods of knocking the blocks down (invent a theory).

4. They knock them down (experimentation)!

5. They learn their own capabilities, learn the reaction of others, conclude through cause and effect (make conclusions).

Here is an example of how inquisitive, investigative preschoolers would solve a problem through the scientific method of inquiry:

1. On a nature walk to collect leaves (they recognize a problem).

2. They think about where to walk, decide which leaves to select based on color, shape, feel, size (collect information).

3. They assume and test different places of collecting leaves and different types of leaves (invent a theory).

4. They gather and examine the leaves, explore the leaves through leaf rubbings (experimentation).

5. They investigate nature through observation and classification of leaves; observe colors, compare shapes and sizes, count leaves, infer similarities and differences (make conclusions).

Leaf Rubbings

You will need: leaves, paper, crayons, a book of nature, curious minds.

What to do:

• Talk about the parts of the leaves: the veins, stems, and different shapes.

• Place the leaves between two pieces of paper.

• Rub the top sheet of paper with a crayon to create the outline of the size and shape of each leaf.

• Rub with crayon until the veins and stem appear.

• Have the children do other types of leaves to compare similarities and differences.

• If possible, find a nature book, a dictionary, or pictures of leaves to compare and determine the types of leaves that have been gathered.

For all methods of inquiry our input can facilitate learning by extending concepts with a verbal exchange of ideas. Linking new words related to a child's activity provokes a word-play association which in itself encourages new words and ideas!

Understanding Biology Through Science Experiments

Children enjoy experimenting and observing the growth and change of living things. The following activities will help the children understand how plants grow.

Planting Seeds

You will need: empty egg cartons—enough for each child, dirt or potting soil, beans or flower seeds (marigolds and lima beans sprout early).

What to do:

- Label each egg carton with a child's name.

- Let the children fill each section up with dirt, and press beans or seeds into each section of dirt.

- Have the children water their plants, and place them near a window.

- Talk about and ask questions about what helps plants grow.

- Use a calendar as an observation graph to record the plant growth each day. Such an experience chart generates questions and discussions. Relate any growth to: sunny days vs. cloudy days; moist soil vs. dry soil; the direction of plant plant growth—upward or downward. Discuss why.

- Incorporate new words: seeds, sprouts, roots, leaves, vines, limbs, branches. Understanding and learning these new words signifies an observable analogy: that children increase their interest and developmental understanding through active learning.

- Read stories about plant growth and changes and related topics such as the sun, water, and seeds.

A small sample of stories about plant growth is:

> Carle, Eric. *The Very Hungry Caterpillar; Jack and the Beanstalk*
> Krauss, Ruth. *The Carrot Seed*
> Lobel, Arnold. *The Rose in My Garden*
> McCloskey, Robert. *Blueberries for Sal*
> Potter, Beatrix. *The Tale of Peter Rabbit*
> Wahl, Jan. *The Cucumber Princess*

Here is another simple experiment to sprout seeds which allows children to *see* the results of plant growth and change, *hear* the language associated with and extending from such an experiment, and actually *do* the experiment themselves (involving taste, smell, and touch).

An Apple Seed Experiment

You will need: small plastic zip-loc® sandwich bags—2 bags for each child, paper towels—cut one piece in half, give each child both pieces, apple seeds (or any fruit seed), magnets.

What to do:

- Let the children have apple slices for a snack and save the seeds.

- Divide the seeds among the children.

- Place some seeds on both pieces of paper towel.

- Place the paper towels in each plastic bag.

- Add a few drops of water to each plastic bag (keep paper towel moist).

- Label each bag with the child's name.

- To observe, learn, and better understand plant growth, let each child place one bag in the freezer and the other bag on the refrigerator with a magnet.

- Add water daily to the paper towels in the freezer and to the bags on the refrigerator.

- Observe and compare any signs of growth between the two bags.

- Add more seeds such as orange or pear to each bag, depending on the snack.

By observing and comparing what happens in each bag over a two month period, the children came to understand that seeds need sunlight and water to sprout. Once their seeds on the refrigerator sprouted, they brought them home to plant in the ground. The active learning involved during that time was not just about sprouting seeds. The conversations that sprouted while checking the seeds added even more to their intellectual growth!

This experiment began in February and was generated by the question, "How do apples grow when the ground is frozen?" The bags in the freezer reinforced that question and led us to discuss, investigate, and read about temperatures, seasons, climates (humid vs. dry), and weather conditions. The question, "Where do apples come from if the ground is frozen?", prompted us to look through nature and geography books. I borrowed books from the library showing weather conditions across the United States. Books with maps of the states and countries introduced various natural landscapes—rain forests, the equator, mountain ranges, farmlands, and deserts. This activity helped the children understand plant life through growth and the factors that affect that growth.

Developing Science Concepts Through Children's Books

Other stories to read that will help develop the concepts of science and language development are:

Bendick, Jeanne. *The Wind*

Brown, Margaret Wise. *The Summer Noisy Book*

Craig, M. Jean. *Spring is Like the Morning*

Darby, Gene. *What is a Season?*

Gorelich, Mary. *Where Does the Butterfly Go When it Rains?*

Goudey, Alice E. *The Day We Saw the Sun Come Up*

Hall, Adelaide. *The Rain Puddle*

Hutchinson, William. *A Child's Book of Sea Shells*

Krauss, Ruth. *The Happy Day*

Parsons, Virginia. *Rain*

Ruchlis, Hy. *How a Rock Came to be in a Fence on a Road Near a Town*

Scheer, Julian. *Rain Makes Applesauce*

Steig, William. *Sylvester and the Magic Pebble*

Swenson, Valerie. *A Child's Book of Stones and Minerals*

Tapio, Pat. *The Lady Who Saw the Good Side of Everything*

Watson, Nancy. *When is Tomorrow?*

Wiese, Kurt. *The Groundhog and His Shadow*

Zolotow, Charlotte. *When the Wind Stops.*

Chapter 13

Understanding Elements of Biology by Caring for Pets and Other Animals

■

Why Care for Animals?

Caring for pets and animals is a natural experience in biological science. Understanding the growth and change in animal life is one area of learning that contributes to the total development of young children. When caring for pets and animals, children can observe their eating habits, sleeping patterns, and basic daily needs. They can learn to be an active participant in caring for and being responsible for an animal; as well as understanding environmental issues through experiences that form relationships with the Earth. Before children can grasp the devastating effects of water pollution, oil spills, deforestation, and unclean air, we have to help them foster a respect for the Earth and the importance of all its living creatures—plants, animals, and humans.

Pets such as fish, turtles, hermit crabs, gerbils, mice, and guinea pigs that are cared for in tanks or aquariums can carry developmentally appropriate experiences and various life learning lessons for young children.

In the lives of young children, taking care of pets offers countless opportunities to learn about different pet needs and behaviors; the feeling of being responsible and knowing you cared for a living thing. An entire curriculum could be built for children involving the care, feeding, and the loving of pets.

Though pet care is generally your responsibility, through questions, sharing information, and discussion children can learn proper methods for feeding, grooming, and the caring of pets by watching you. Your questions will spark their interest; their interest leads to teachable moments.

❏ **IF,** for instance, as you near the fish tank you ask the children, "What did you eat for breakfast?";

❏ **THEN** each child is eager to get a chance to recall their breakfast or make up the silliest, most non-nutritious one.

❏ **HOW?** Get them thinking with more questions: "Can our goldfish go to the supermarket to buy that for breakfast?"

❏ **WHY?** Phrasing questions such as this one helps children develop their thinking skills. Though the answer is a simple one, it presents the inference of how dependent pets really are on us to feed and care for them. "What do you suppose fish do like to eat?" Give each child a chance to guess. Then read some of the ingredients listed on the fish food container: wheat flour, meat meal, fish meal, shrimp meal, wheat germ meal, dried yeast, crab meat.

At this point the children can start to make analogies.

❏ **IF** you begin talking about some of the cereals they enjoy for breakfast being made of wheat flour or wheat germ;

❏ **THEN** using the similarities becomes an effective learning tool. Ask if they too have ever eaten meals of meat, fish, shrimp, or crabmeat.

❏ **HOW?** Create other analogies. Ask the children to think about what they do when they get hungry or how they get their food. Let them pretend they are fish swimming in water looking for food. Children know fish swim in water. Any other resemblances went unnoticed, were never observed, never considered. Questions help children focus on thinking things through and seeing resemblances of themselves.

❑ **WHY?** Making analogies offers a general teaching procedure you can use with children learning about pets. Help children learn through observations, discussions, and experiences that look at similarities and differences between themselves and a pet. Children will learn that pets are a lot like themselves requiring regular health care and plenty of love and attention.

■

"Can I Feed It Yet?"

Seeing similarities and recognizing differences helps children learn to ask their own questions. Pet feeding habits can be observed, discussed, shared, and read about. Children can learn about animals that prefer meat and those that favor vegetables. Reading stories like Beatrix Potter's *Peter Rabbit* would open the topic of feeding habits up to discussions about the favorite meals of animals and the meat vs. vegetable preferences of the children.

■

"When Will It Come Up for Air?"

❑ **IF** you ask the children to think about different breathing techniques;

❑ **THEN** begin talking about land animals and water animals and animals that can breathe on land and in water.

❑ **HOW?** Through books and with stories such as Leo Lionni's *Fish is Fish*. Tadpoles make a good, interesting study. Beginning as fish-like creatures with long tails, breathing through gills, tadpoles eventually develop legs and lungs and transform into frogs with disappearing tails. Fairy tales like *The Frog Prince* and the story of *The Dancing Frog* by Quentin Blake lend to the enchantment between children and frogs.

□ **WHY?** You can find a whole world of fascinating knowledge in a pond. Concentrate on the breathing techniques of various, different animals to develop language and thought. By letting the children focus on and compare the different breathing methods of animals, children can learn about beaks, nostrils, noses, gills, and lungs. Learn even more new words as you show and ask the children if they know how to "inhale" and "exhale." Make a chart of different animal characteristics and have the children find stuffed animals or cut out pictures of animals that could match the characteristics on the chart.

■

"Where Does It Live?"

Nonfiction books in the children's library can answer that question for you. These books contain wonderful pictures showing various animal homes and nesting patterns. They offer a whole lesson of new words for language development that help children understand how different animals live or need to be cared for.

Children can look at tree-nesters; cliff dwellers; ground-nesters; a cocoon or a protective chrysalis; nest holes; dams, lodges, and larders; marsupial pouches like that of a kangaroo and animals that nestle their young chicks like the Emperor penguins. You can look at ant farms; tunnels; burrows; dens; and caves and share all of this information together.

Looking at animals in a broader view may help children realize that we are responsible not only for our pets but for all animals in the world.

□ **IF** some of the children would like to pretend to be baby animals that will need food and a place to live;

□ **THEN** cut the corners off of large sheets of news-print paper into the shape of an egg.

□ **HOW?** Give each "baby animal" child one piece of egg-shaped newsprint paper. Ask them to curl up onto their egg pretending to be baby animals ready to hatch and then wanting to be fed. Let the other children pretend to be the parent animals ready to feed their babies. Have the children reverse their roles of babies and parents.

❑ **WHY?** It becomes easy to see that just like children, animals need homes and family to protect them and keep them comfortable, warm, sometimes dry, and always safe. Pets require the same amount of care.

Next, think about some animals that carry their homes with them like snails, clams, turtles, and hermit crabs. Recently, land hermit crabs became a very popular household pet. General knowledge about hermit crabs, for example, will come from information you may already have acquired or need to read about and then relay to the children. While looking for a pet care book on hermit crabs, Ron Roy, author of several children's books, peaked my curiosity with the title of his pet care book: *What Has Ten Legs and Eats Corn Flakes?*

Roy offers step-by-step information on how to prepare, clean, and maintain an aquarium for pet hermit crabs.

What to put in the food dish, alongside the necessary water dish: lettuce, bread, crackers, cookies and, of course, the cornflakes. (All of the children can relate to that menu.) There is even special food for land hermit crabs available at pet stores.

We learned from this book that crabs like room temperatures not too hot nor too cold. Actively involving the children in deciding on a safe place for the aquarium helped them to remember to keep the aquarium away from too sunny a window, a radiator, or even the air conditioner.

The most fun and interesting behavior to learn and observe about the hermit crab is selecting and purchasing extra, bigger shells. The land hermit crabs need the bigger shells to move into as they grow.

What Can Turtles Teach?

Not only do turtles carry their homes on their bodies like the hermit crabs, they carry a wonderful early childhood educational lesson: learn not to be too aggressive while trying to learn how to defend yourself.

Though we tend to associate turtles with water, we found two box turtles strolling down the street! We knew they weren't safe there so we brought them home in a box with intentions to put them back into the woods. Instead we placed them in an empty fish tank and began feeding them lettuce, worms, and strawberries.

One of the turtles died shortly thereafter and we had a proper burial close to where we dig for their worms. According to Marzollo and Lloyd (1972) the death of any pet should be dealt with honestly and directly and as completely as you can.

The children still love to dig in the dirt and as soon as they come across a worm they immediately want to give it to the surviving turtle. Though reluctantly, even their parents doing weekend gardening work have admitted to storing the worms they find in their children's pails for their children to bring back to my house on Monday for the pet turtle.

Caring for the turtle is easy. It is still in the empty fish tank except for the place it likes to sun itself and the flat dish of water it likes to soak itself in. Watching it retract when we come near but then peak out from curiosity is fun. It seems to constantly search for food during the warmer season. According to the Reader Digest's book *The ABC's of Nature* (1985), turtles are not active in the cold. As cold weather approaches, land turtles bury themselves under leaves or soil and aquatic turtles lie dormant in the mud of lakes and ponds. Since our turtle lives indoors all year round we have found it does seem to eat less in the colder months but still enjoys a fly, mealy-bug, or worms now and then even in the winter.

❏ **IF** you or the children are not particularly fond of catching flies or digging for worms for a turtle;

❏ **THEN** pet stores generally carry mealy-bugs and earthworms for turtles to eat. Pet shop workers are very informative.

❏ **HOW?** We asked about new food suggestions to feed our turtle and received a list of new ideas which included raw hamburger (which our turtle doesn't care for), chopped apples without the skin, and a special caution about not feeding the turtle the apple seeds which are poisonous to a turtle.

❏ **WHY?** Hearing this just made me wonder about the consequences of innocently introducing and feeding pets and animals unhealthy food choices. Fortunately the library has a section on pet and animal care. Browsing through a few of the turtle books, I came across *The Total Turtle* (1975) by Martha Emilie Reeves. The book contains a list of plants that are poisonous to a turtle.

During a visit to the pet store while we were looking for a new turtle to keep this one company, we heard that baby turtles carry salmonella, which can cause serious intestinal infections in humans. Again, *The Total Turtle* was consulted. Reeves advises that since 1972 state laws prohibit the sale of turtles under four inches in length and forbids importation of turtles under that size. These laws have helped eliminate the danger of salmonella.

❏ **IF** children are allowed to be actively involved in the caring, loving, feeding, grooming, and training of pets;

❏ **THEN** the understanding, empathy, proper attention, and love a pet requires will become a pleasant learning experience.

■
"Do Pets Have to Take Naps, Too?"

This innocent question offers keen insight. Children can readily observe pet dogs and cats stretching, getting comfortable, and curling up preparing themselves to take a restful nap. Resting is one of a cat's favorite activities.

There are pet dogs and cats that are wonderful playmates for children; however, even the best pet among a group of children may become too excited. The fast motions of too many children may cause an animal to feel threatened. At this point you may need to have the children leave the pet alone so it can calm down and rest up for the next play time. Children have to learn that pets have rights and feelings that must be respected.

■
Hibernation—Talk About a Nap!

After reading Crockett Johnson's *Will Spring Be Early or Will Spring Be Late?* on Ground Hog Day, the children hid under a big blanket and pretended to be hibernating ground hogs. I turned off the lights. While I was shining a flashlight (the sun) on their blanket (their burrow) they pretended to wake from a long winter's nap and clamor around searching for food. One by one their heads appeared out from under the blanket to discover their shadows (and six more weeks of winter) or to decide to search for food (and the coming of an early spring).

With activities where children are actively learning particular animal behavior, introducing new words becomes easier to understand. Words like hibernation, camouflage, molting, and preening just roll out delightfully in the right context.

"Can I Wash It in the Bathtub?"

Children get accustomed to and therefore learn very early that a regular routine for their own cleanliness is important and necessary. So it would be quite understandable to hear a child ask such a question concerning an animal or their pet.

Common household pets such as mice, gerbils, hamsters, and especially cats can clean themselves. In a National Geographic Society book, *Helping Our Animal Friends,* photographs show children gently scrubbing their friendly pony and other pictures show a calm looking cocker spaniel sitting in a basin of warm, soapy water with children cleaning its skin and hair to rid it of fleas. Some of the pictures are of children grooming their pet with the help of a 4-H Club worker. In many areas 4-H Clubs help children learn how to clean, groom, and train their animals with prescribed methods of care.

With all pet care you can concentrate on explaining how a pet cage or aquarium is a mini-ecosystem for the well-being of the animal inside it. Hopefully your message will impart that just as we learn to be responsible for these mini-environments being clean, cared for, and properly maintained for the well-being of the pet; so too do we need to feel responsible for our own environment and for the well-being of all living things.

Extending Concepts of Pet Care with Children's Literature

Extend concepts of pet care through stories:

Fiction:
Allen, Marjorie N. *One, 2, 3—Ah-Choo*
Chalmers, Mary. *6 Dogs, 23 Cats, 45 Mice and 116 Spiders*

Kellogg, Steven. *Can I Keep Him?*
Lenski, Lois. *Debbie and Her Pets*
Lionni, Leo. *Fish is Fish*
Mayer, Mercer. *Just Me and My Puppy*
Potter, Beatrix. *Peter Rabbit*
Viorst, Judith. *The Tenth Good Thing About Barney*
Zimmerman, Nathan. *Positively No Pets Allowed*

Nonfiction:
Marzollo, Jean, and Janice Lloyd. *Learning Through Play*
McPherson, Mark. *Choosing Your Pet*
Reader's Digest *ABC's of Nature, A Family Answer Book*
Rinard, Judith E. *Helping Our Animal Friends* (National Geographic Society)
Roy, Ron. *What Has Ten Legs and Eats Corn Flakes?*

■

Understanding Elements of Environmental Science Through Bird Watching

Be mindful that some children just can't seem to enjoy the feel of fingerpaints or the squishing of shaving cream between their fingers, never mind digging in dirt and handling worms. Petting or holding an animal does not come easily for some children. But the message of caring for the environment is an important one for all. Designing activities and learning experiences around the observation of birds appeals to all children yet still respects the distance required by other children. Playing and learning outside makes the environmental message even easier to understand.

Feeding the Birds

The simplest, most fun, informative, direct learning experience that introduces children to the biological science of animals is to let them feed the birds! Stand outside, throw birdseed or bread crumbs out for the birds, move far back, crouch down, wait, and watch! Most birds will come to investigate within a few minutes.

I have a large poster of different types of birds. I lie it on the ground and the children sit around it. We talk (especially in whispers), and try to figure out if any of the birds we have observed match the birds on the poster.

These simple observations have lead to discussions revolving around the various colors of each bird, which undoubtedly increases our fascination. We have observed black birds with colors only on their wings. We wonder how these colorful birds use camouflage. We've traced the tappings of a woodpecker and found it circling a tree. We listen to birds communicate and try to imagine what they could possibly be talking about. One morning Caitlin and Tyler became completely absorbed in listening to birds chirping. Almost as a reflex action, they began chirping aloud, right back to a bird. It was as if they were trying to answer it directly. Playfully, I asked what the bird was asking them. Tyler said, "The bird is chirping, 'Thank you'." Caitlin said the birds sounded "happy for the food." And she promptly reminded me to not to forget to feed the fish. (Bird songs and/or calls often offer easy ways to identify birds. The Audubon Society has a two album set that is available at your local library.)

From the poster and related resource materials, we have compared birds that fly with types of birds that swim. We also try to visually discriminate types of birds by their size and wonder how big the baby birds in that nest could be.

The Readers Digest book of *Birds • Their Life • Their Ways • Their World* offers colorful illustrations and interesting facts ranging from owls to flamingos. Check your local library for other good bird books.

Making Bird Feeders

Another simple activity that instills the value of feeling responsible in a relationship with the Earth and its living things is helping children make their own bird feeders.

A Homemade Bird Feeder

You will need: jar lids; any size, one for each child. One hammer and nail will do nicely; and long pieces of yarn or string, enough for each child.

What to do:

• Let the children, with your supervision, hammer the nail through the center of their jar lid.

• Tie a knot at one end of each piece of yarn or string.

• Have the children push their piece of yarn or string through the nail hole.

• Make a loop for them at the other end of the yarn or string and let the children hang their bird feeders outside on different tree branches.

• Have them fill the lid with bread crumbs or birdseed.

• Stand back and birdwatch! (Don't let their bird feeders dangle too low to the ground or it will become a handy bird trap for cats to play with instead.)

Seasonal Bird Feeders

Encourage the children to build snowmen on snowy days. Besides the sheer fun of playing outdoors in the snow, building the snowman itself is a physical activity for large muscle development. Our snowmen definitely serve a social purpose because everyone is encouraged to contribute to the team effort. Planning the actual construction allows everyone to be an active member of the group.

Over the past few years the children have raised their standards—even for the snowman! Their snowmen must also "feel" productive. The older children want the snowman to serve as a birdfeeder because they understand the effects of winter on food sources from other hands-on activities, discussions, and books. So they now ask for raisins to use for buttons; cookie crumbs for eyes; sunflower seeds make good teeth, and various pieces of dry cereals create interesting hairstyles. Any crumb or sandwich crust left uneaten at lunch gets incorporated into the construction of their snowman. And their tradition is being passed along to the younger children who have been observing, helping, and learning from the older children daily.

■

An Initiation to Environmental Discoveries

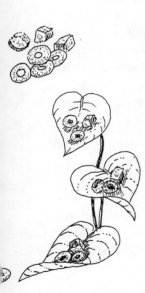

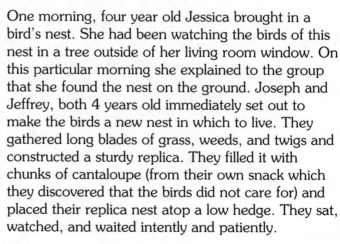

One morning, four year old Jessica brought in a bird's nest. She had been watching the birds of this nest in a tree outside of her living room window. On this particular morning she explained to the group that she found the nest on the ground. Joseph and Jeffrey, both 4 years old immediately set out to make the birds a new nest in which to live. They gathered long blades of grass, weeds, and twigs and constructed a sturdy replica. They filled it with chunks of cantaloupe (from their own snack which they discovered that the birds did not care for) and placed their replica nest atop a low hedge. They sat, watched, and waited intently and patiently.

I wanted to help the two and three year old children participate in this caring process. By feeding, protecting, and providing shelter for "Jessica's birds," the children were innocently initiating an invaluable lesson. To help with this process, I found an old frozen bagel tucked away in the freezer and I diced it into small pieces. I mixed together a flour and water paste and gave each child a paintbrush. Each child "painted" a leaf outside with this paste mixture and placed a piece of their bagel on it. The children wanted and believed their actions were directly intended for Jessica's evicted birds. We came back into the house and watched the birds from the windows. Jessica felt a loss. She shared her sorrow with her friends and they responded admirably. This is a total learning experience: children involved, actively learning physically, socially, intellectually, and emotionally.

■

Extending Environmental Activities Through Children's Books

Reading stories and books about animals and related environmental activities to children provides a culmination of new scientific thought: what Elliot Eisner (as cited in Brandt, 1988) calls conceptual bridges. An important thinking skill necessary at any level of development is the construction of conceptual bridges. Relating and integrating previously learned facts and feelings to understand new, discerning experiences of active learning. These conceptual bridges generate values, more ways of thinking, language development, and learning. A selection of good books to choose from includes:

Aardema, Verna. *Who's in Rabbit's House?*
Barrett, Judi. *Animals Should Definitely Not Wear Clothing*
Bornstein, Ruth. *Little Gorilla*
Brown, Margaret Wise. *The Runaway Bunny*
Busch, Phyllis S. *Once There Was a Tree*
Carle, Eric. *The Very Hungry Caterpillar; The Robber and the Honeybee*
Cherry, Lynne. *The Great Kapok Tree*
deRegniers, Beatrice S. *May I Bring a Friend?*

Dr. Seuss. *The Lorax*

Flack, Marjorie. *Angus and the Cats; Angus and the Ducks; Ask Mr. Bear*

Freeman, Don. *Corduroy*

Gàg, Wanda. *Millions of Cats*

Keats, Ezra Jack. *The Snowy Day*

Kessler, Ethel and Leonard. *Do Bears Sit in Chairs?*

Krauss, Ruth. *The Happy Day*

Leaf, Munro. *The Story of Ferdinand*

Lionni, Leo. *Fish is Fish; Swimmy; Frederick; A Color of His Own*

Mizumura, Kazue. *If I Built a Village*

Munari, Bruno. *Bruno Munari's Zoo*

Noguere, Suzanne, and Tony Chen. *Little Koala*

Rice, Eve. *Sam Who Never Forgets*

Silverstein, Shel. *The Giving Tree*

Wildsmith, Brian. *Animal Games; Animal Homes; Birds; Fishes; Squirrels; Wild Animals; The Lazy Bear*

Williams, Garth. *The Rabbit's Wedding*

Zalken, Jan Breskin. *Will You Count The Stars Without Me?*

All of these activities will increase young children's learning about their natural, real world through their own active participation. We can help them learn by allowing them to think and do—physically, socially, intellectually, and emotionally. And they will still be eager to learn more!

Once children become actively involved with their immediate surroundings, they begin to see things around them differently. They become more observant, more open-minded; they learn to ask questions and to reason better. Children then begin to understand how to be critical of the effects of human behavior towards the Earth.

Chapter 14

Human Life: Learning About Growth and Change

■

Exploring Relationships Through Active Learning

❑ **IF** you are caring for an infant,

❑ **THEN** engage the other children in that care.

❑ **HOW?** By letting them be active participants in the necessary details of caring and loving the baby: encourage children to play gently with the baby; ask children to talk and sing to the baby.

❑ **WHY?** Encouraging children to "help" you take care of the baby develops their sense of self-esteem and worth. They come to learn how to care for and feel responsible toward other people—you and the baby. Babies respond eagerly and enthusiastically to the playful antics of children. The baby's attention makes the children attentive to baby. They form a mutual, reciprocal accord. If the baby fusses children are quick to respond with a toy, a dance, or a smile. Young children are curious about their own life's history. Seeing a baby fed and cuddled and cared for is a perfect analogy for children to make distinct references to understand their own history. They are really interested in how they were fed, cuddled, and cared for. Seeing you care for a baby invites questions and discussions about how they were fed. What did they eat? When could they talk? When did they walk?

Rival moments may occur when the baby is viewed as a wedge between you and the children. But if the children can learn that you accept and expect their help and cooperation in any form you see necessary, their responsiveness and attentiveness remain intact.

They feel better about themselves and you can appreciate them even more being around babies.

Watching a baby babble and play is a fascinating experience for young children—especially for children who do not have younger brothers or sisters. There are stories and books about babies that all children enjoy hearing. For the children with siblings, hearing such stories may allay their feelings and emotions they can't quite understand about this new life. Some of these books are:

Alexander, Martha. *Nobody Asked Me If I Wanted a Baby Sister; When The Baby Comes, I'm Moving Out*
Hagen, Barbara Shook. *Gorilla Wants to Be the Baby*
Hoban, Russell. *A Baby Sister for Frances*
Jarrell, Mary. *The Knee-Baby*
Keats, Ezra Jack. *Peter's Chair*
Scott, Ann Herbert. *On Mother's Lap*
Stein, Sara Bonneth. *That New Baby*
Steptoe, John. *Stevie*
Zolotow, Charlotte. *Do You Know What I'll Do?*

When you share a book with a child, you are saying, in effect, that their feelings are natural and you are willing to help children understand themselves and their relationships with others.

■

Understanding Our Anatomy Through Play

Children make their first discoveries about themselves through their bodies. Their senses and emotions are all entwined. A direct approach to playfully learn more about their bodies comes in a modified version of the game Twister®.

Learning Body Parts

You will need: the Twister® mat, the Twister® Spinner, and 2, 3, and 4 year old children who can match or recognize red, yellow, blue, and green.

How to play:

• Spin the spinner, and call out, "Hand on red!", "Foot on blue!" (Remember that developmentally, 2, 3, and 4 year olds are not expected to understand left and right. The purpose of this game is to learn to understand different body parts through play.)

• Spin again, and call out "Nose on yellow!"

• Spin again, and call out these playful commands: "Knee on green!", "Elbow on blue!", "Ear on red!"

What better way can children playfully learn body parts like ankle, wrist, shoulders, or spine? They are learning the importance of their own bodies. They are not only learning about their bodies, they are learning to listen, to wait, to anticipate, to play. They are learning how to play together.

If you are working with even younger children, create a simpler version of the Twister® game by overlooking the color matching to just get a finger, nose, or an ear on a circle.

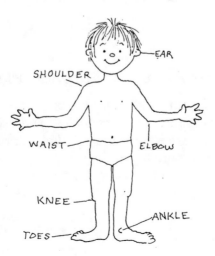

A Tracing Activity

You will need: brown paper bags cut open to lie flat, and the youngsters.

What to do:

- Ask a child to lie down on the bag. Trace the outline of their body.
- Let the children fill in their details: eyes, ears, nose, hair, hands, feet.
- Call out different body parts and ask the children to find them. (They may point to their own bodies or to those on the bag.)

Another modified version for any age is to ask the children to stand in front of a mirror. As you call out parts of the body have the children point to that part on their own body. They tend to get silly making wild funny faces at themselves and each other in the mirror. This leads to another example of learning through play: expressing feelings through facial expressions and body language. Their bodies and minds are amazingly accurate and perceptive. Follow up the facial expressions with questions such as why and when people make that particular face.

■

Developing a Self-Image

Four 3 year olds asked me to trace their body outlines. Given markers they not only drew in their own body parts, they sketched in shirts, skirts, pants, socks, shoes, belts, necklaces, earrings, hats, eyelashes, and nostrils! The children have asked to do this activity repeatedly. We have since added their weight and height to each outline to increase their self-esteem and self-awareness.

Learning Through the Senses

Children grow and learn through the use of their senses. They learn early that various objects have different sounds, smells, tastes, and textures. You have already provoked this learning and can help children distinguish such differences through experimentation. All sensory experimentation increases language development and conceptual awareness. The following activities encompass the senses of smell, sound, taste, touch, and vision.

Smell

You will need any of the following items: soap, perfume, air freshener, coffee, maple syrup, orange slices, vinegar, cinnamon, peppermint.

What to do:

• Let the children see the household products.

• Ask the children to close their eyes.

• Pass a household product or grocery item under their nose to sniff.

• Ask each child to guess what they think it smells like.

Sound

You will need: a portable tape recorder and cassette tape.

What to do:

• Walk around your house and record the sounds that surround you. Take the tape recorder outdoors to record the daily sounds: a knock at the door, a door slam, a clock chime, a baby's rattle, typewriter keys, a toilet bowl flush, cars and trucks passing by, water running, dogs barking, lawnmowers, birds chirping . . . whatever you hear!

• Play it back for the children to guess what sounds they hear.

• Daily sounds, like music, often go unnoticed. Listening for sounds forms concepts and mental images of commonplace items and activities that are not often appreciated. Guessing the sounds generates a tremendous amount of language stimulation, development, and learning.

Taste

You will need: an assortment of common, recognizable foods: dry cereal, popcorn, peanuts, grapes, raisins, cheese chunks, bagel chips, crackers.

What to do:

• Ask the children to close their eyes and feed them each a piece of food. (Seeing the choices to be tasted first aids in group participation.)

• Can they guess what they ate?

• Let them taste test a different choice and try to guess again.

Texture

You will need: various household objects in a bag or pillowcase: table-spoons, cup, tennis ball, cotton ball, toys of different sizes and textures.

What to do:

• Gather your group of children.

• Depending on their ages and verbal skills, decide if they need to see the objects first.

• Ask one child at a time to reach into the bag or pillowcase to feel one item and try to guess what it is before taking it out.

Sand Painting

You will need: glue, sand, paper or cardboard.

What to do:

• Let the children squirt glue onto their paper or cardboard, and spread it around with a paintbrush. (Be sure to rinse the paintbrush.)

• Next have them sprinkle sand all over their paper or cardboard.

• Let the glue dry and shake off the excess sand.

Vision: Making Transparencies

You will need: wax paper, collectibles, an iron.

What to do:

• Arrange things like leaves between two pieces of wax paper.

• Press with a warm iron on both sides of wax paper.

• Glue ribbons, colored cut-up pieces of paper, or Styrofoam peanuts around the edges for a frame. Punch a hole through the top to hang.

Other activities you can do to explore the sense of vision are: Provide magnifying glasses for the children to use; this encourages them to experiment on their own. Play with kaleidoscopes or explore the house with the children to find things that are transparent (i.e., windows, tracing paper, plastic bags, colored glass, cellophane paper, glass bottles).

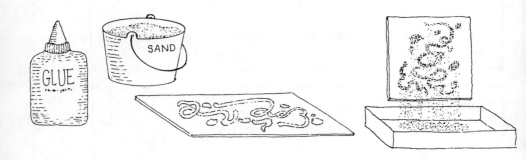

Chapter 15

Physical Science

■

Fun with Chemistry

Children possess a certain amount of curiosity and their ability to investigate phenomena should be encouraged. As a result, active scientific learning takes place.

One morning, the children were outside blowing bubbles. This activity in itself incorporates social, emotional, individual, physical, and intellectual challenges. All ages are involved. The older children even take time out to blow bubbles for the toddlers to chase.

Each child had a cup of homemade bubble liquid—dish detergent and water—and blowing wands. I brought out straws and toothpicks. The children as "scientists" did this project: blowing bubbles in their cups and piercing the bubbles with toothpicks. I added baby powder to their bubble water. They continued to blow cloudy white bubbles. However, as "chemists" they soon discovered with the talcum powder added the bubbles *do not* burst when pierced with the toothpick! (With the powder the water's surface tension increases making the bubbles more difficult to burst.)

The children were surprised and excited at this discovery and it made them eager to experiment and learn more. This chapter concentrates on activities that will encourage children to become active learners about the world they live in.

Learning About the Seasons

Help the children become aware of different seasons through discussions and stories. A day doesn't go by without a child reporting on the weather: "I needed to wear my boots today." One way of letting children see and play with the seasons is to cut out a wide assortment of pictures from catalogues and magazines. Include:

• Clothing—from bathing suits to ski wear.

• Sporting Scenes—baseball games, beaches (show swimmers and surfers), skiing, sleighriding scenes.

• Equipment—lawnmowers, tents, rowboats, skis, kites, surfboards, tubes.

• Landscapes—fields in full bloom, snowcapped mountains, snow scenes, deserts.

Once you have gathered a good assortment of pictures depicting summer or winter, draw a set of overlapping circles. Label each circle:

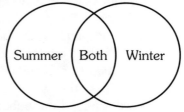

Begin by asking the children to look at a picture to decide if it belongs in the summer set or the winter set. Some pictures could apply to both seasons and the children place them in the subset section.

Use this same "set" format to play "Inside or Outside." Cut out pictures of familiar objects and clothing. Let the children decide if the pictures belong "Inside or Outside." Our set of pictures includes: carpeting, fireplaces, furniture, a piano, a toaster, beds, swimming pools, patio furniture, golf clubs, skis, a lawnmower, cars, an ocean liner, and airplanes. Some of the pictures belong in the subset:

shoes, watches, paper cups and plates, shirts.

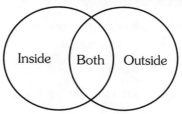

Inside   Both   Outside

■

Re-Creating Fall's Foliage

Watching the leaves change color in autumn is an experiment in itself. Re-creating these colorful leaves connects art with science.

Creating Fall Colors

You will need: an assortment of the most colorful leaves, green construction paper, a Spin Art toy (Ohio Art, nasta toy co., approximately $9.99), and paints.

What to do:

• Cut out a crude shape of a leaf from the green construction paper.

• Place it on the Spin Art tray.

• Let the children add the paints to the spinning tray to re-create the changing colors of fall.

■

Understanding Temperature

Children gather information by seeing and comparing similarities and differences. One experiment that shows children that materials expand (become larger) when heated, and contract (become smaller) when cooled uses the heat energy of a sunny day.

An Experiment for a Sunny Day

You will need: empty glass bottles (enough for all, if possible), balloons, and a sunny day.

What to do:

• Place the balloons around the rims of the glass bottles.

• Let the children decide if they want to place their bottles in a sunny spot or in the shade.

• After a short time compare the differences in the balloons. The balloons on the bottles in the sun will appear slightly blown up from heat expansion. The balloons on the bottles in the shade remain deflated.

■

Experiments with Melting Ice

On cold, wintry days where children can still see icy sidewalks and slippery front steps. Ask the children what people can do to make sidewalks and streets safe. Then let them see for themselves.

An Ice Activity

You will need: small dishes and enough ice cubes for each child.

What to do:

• Give each child a dish with an ice cube in it.

• Let them pass around salt shakers to sprinkle salt onto their ice cubes. They will watch as the salt dissolves the ice. If you have rock salt let them spoon a little of it onto their ice cube. Explain that with this mineral people salt the sidewalks and streets to dissolve ice to make walking and driving conditions safer.

• This is a hands-on approach to problem solving, where children can see and understand results. (This is a fun activity no matter where you may live!)

■

Making Your Own Rainbow

On sunny days, leave a clear glass bowl of water and a package of small baguette mirrors (under $2.00 in hardware stores) on a sunny table. The "experimenters" position the bowl of water to where the sun can shine directly on it. They experiment by placing mirrors in the water and outside of the bowl to try to catch the sunlight. Wiggling, curving, and streaking rainbows appear on the ceiling and walls. This activity and other fun activities of this type can be found in a book by Dinah Moché called *Magic Science Tricks*.

■

The Shadow Experiment

Our shadows are fun to chase! Or run to catch another child's shadow! Or experiment to see how tall you can make your own shadow. Or position yourself to be very small.

Children can play and dance with their shadows. Have them draw pictures tracing a shadow. This is another good activity relating art with science.

"Can your very own personal shadow move even if you don't?" Throw that question out to your group. You'll be surprisingly amazed at the wide range of answers you will receive! Hopefully someone will say, "Let's experiment!"

For this experiment you will need curious youngsters, a sunny day, and a piece of chalk. Take the experimenters outside at mid-morning. Line them up side-by-side across the sidewalk or a driveway to cast their shadows. Draw a chalk line across the head of each child's shadow. Label each shadow with the child's name. Go back outdoors after lunch and ask the children to find their names on their sidewalk shadow.

Now they cast another shadow so draw another chalk line. They are in the same space, but are their shadows? Try it. It's fun to find out!

Rocks and Pebbles

On our walks, it is inevitable that one child, if not all of the children, will come back with a rock collection. Everyone spreads their collection out on the sidewalk or front steps to compare and admire their treasured possessions. They talk about the shapes, the shading and color, the rough edges, and smooth surfaces. I give them each a piece of paper with their name printed in the corner and a small zip-loc® sandwich bag stapled on under their name. I draw the "set" format onto their papers.

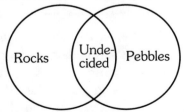

They separate the large stones from the smaller ones. They further subdivide the rough edged rocks from the smooth pebbles. They are able to classify, observe, continue talking and comparing, and then save their collection in the sandwich bag to take home. The children learn to differentiate the rough feel of rocks from the smooth feel of pebbles through seeing, feeling, and comparing. They also learn about natural science.

To extend the activity further, the library has numerous informative, richly illustrated books classifying rocks and minerals for you to share with the children.

■

Learning About Erosion

Children learn by comparing and observing similarities and differences. This activity provides a subtle lesson to remind us how powerful we are in determining what happens to our environment.

In a good pile of backyard dirt or park sandbox, learning about erosion comes easily. Ask the children to build a large mound of dirt or sand. With cups or pitchers, let them pour water slowly over the mound and watch how fast the mound disappears. Now ask them to rebuild the mound of dirt or sand, but this time stick leaves, twigs, and grass into the mound. Pour the water again over the dirt or sand and observe the difference. The children learn first hand how the plant life protects and saves the Earth.

Dinosaurs! Dinosaurs! Dinosaurs!

Two hundred seventy million years ago is a difficult concept for *anyone* to comprehend! But the fascination with dinosaurs and all the related names, words, and terminology proves that young children can learn about any subject if they show interest and if it is presented in a developmentally appropriate context.

Stories, dinosaur games, building models, playing with dinosaur figures, building dinosaur caves out of blocks or clay, and molding Play-Doh® onto dinosaur figures are only some of the activities the children could experience to help them come to know and understand dinosaurs.

Searching for Fossils

As "archeologists" the 3, 4, and 5 year old children were one day thoroughly absorbed pretending their "work" involved digging up fossils in the backyard dirt and sand area. Seeing such intense interest and determination, I decided to make their efforts come to a realization.

I mixed a cup of Plaster of Paris and enough cold water to form a pliable paste. I plopped twelve teaspoons of this mixture out onto a piece of waxed paper. To create the "fossils" I pressed fork tines into a couple, dragged a comb over a few, pressed a thumb on some, and created different designs (bones) on the rest.

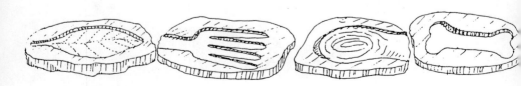

And then I buried the "fossils" in their "archeological dig,"—without the children knowing! What excitement they created! Who would have guessed digging for fossils in your own backyard could be just as thrilling as discovering a long lost buried treasure? To "archeologists" fossils are buried treasures.

Once everyone had found a few fossils, they knew they had to be taken to the laboratory (an idea from a recently read story) for the "paleontologists" to figure out the origin of the fossils.

From all of these hands-on "scientific" experiences and experiments the children will not only develop language skills with vocabulary words and related conceptual cues, and associable qualities of a social science; but they will also develop a finer, tangible relationship in the nature of the world.

PART FIVE

Math

Chapter 16

Preliminary Math Skills

■

Early Math Discoveries

In the sensorimotor stage of development (from birth to 2 years old) infants and toddlers play with objects to discover what can roll, what they can move, what can stack, and what fits together. These early discoveries are forming conceptual bridges; the initial concepts of math and logical thinking. Many of these mathematical concepts are found in the daily, playful activities the children get themselves involved in: matching, grouping, opposites, shapes, sizes, patterns, sharing, weights, comparing, re-arranging, and measuring. Through these daily interactions and activities children will learn about counting and number recognition. As caregivers we promote and provoke this learning as an extension of child's play with a wide arrangement of experiences.

■

Developing Memory Skills Through Play

The following activities are helpful for children to observe, remember, think, identify, learn, and play.

❏ **IF** you want to help children observe details, sharpen their memory skills, use their minds to think, learn new words, and learn a new game to play;

❏ **THEN** play What's Missing?

❏ **HOW?** Gather five or six items such as: spoon, pencil, spatula, paintbrush, paperclip, envelope.

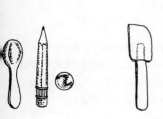

1. Place each item on the table. Let each child talk about the items before they play the game to be sure they are familiar with the items and can relate to them.

2. Have each child take a turn saying out loud the name of each item. Point to each item as they say the name. Always point and start with the same item so each child can form a mental pattern of the position each item is in before playing.

3. The first child to play turns around to face *away* from the objects on the table.

4. Remove one of the items. Hold and hide it under the table. Remind the other children *not to tell* the player which one is missing!

5. Call the player back to the table and ask if they know what's missing. If the child does not seem to remember, offer clues. Use the same words you used to describe and explain what each item was before playing to help them recall. Don't shake the child's confidence! If they still can't remember ask the other children to help the player guess.

6. Use the same items for each child's turn. Do *not* change or rotate the positions of the items. As each child takes a turn the mental imagery of the objects is formulating. Let the imagery gel before changing positions or replacing items or even adding more.

❏ **WHY?** Before children can really understand what numbers are and what numbers mean, experiences with mathematical/logical concepts have to help children match, sort, and classify objects. Activities must help children realize characteristics that make objects, and people, same/and/or different. Math requires memory. To understand and learn how to "do math" children have to learn to think critically in order to solve problems. They need you to respect, accept, and encourage individual thoughts. You need to develop their self-confidence and their willingness to take risks and leaps toward learning.

❏ **IF** you have one bag of assorted nuts;

❏ **THEN** play Sorting Assorted Nuts.

❏ **HOW?** Empty the bag into a large bowl. There are usually four types of nuts in one bag—almonds, walnuts, pecans, and filberts. (Let only four children play at one time to avoid the confusion of sharing one type of nut between children.)

Talk about the color, shape, and texture of each nutshell. Give each child a bowl or cup and place one kind of nut in each child's bowl. Ask the children to take all of the nuts that are the same as the one in their bowl out of the large bowl.

When all of the nuts are sorted share information about the kind they each had to sort; share time describing how the shells are all different—smooth, rough, with holes, with lines, the largest, the smallest, roundness and so on.

■

Bowling For All Ages

You will need an inexpensive plastic bowling ball and a ten pin toy set or a small ball with blocks to knock down in order to play. Different aspects of bowling are suitable for every age.

NAME	1st turn / 2nd turn	1st turn / 2nd turn	1st turn / 2nd turn
Joseph 5 yrs.	3 / 4		
LAUREN 4 YRS. 10 MOS.	7 / 1		
Jeff 4 yrs. 3 mos.	— / ×		
Jessica 4 YRS. 10 mos.	4 / 5		
MATT 15 mos.	8 / —		
Emily 8 mos.	3 / 2		

1. Let the older children decide who goes first, second . . . , let them include the infants and toddlers in their ranking. Why? To develop values. You are showing the older children that you trust their efforts and judgments to help organize the game.

2. List the names of all the children playing in the order they have decided upon.

3. Explain how to play: Roll the bowling ball to knock down as many bowling pins as possible.

Everyone gets two turns. Ask them to count how many pins are knocked down on their first turn (or count with you). Write in their score. Roll the ball again. Count. Write in the second score.

Let the infants and toddlers play! A baby able to sit can be placed in front of the pins. Talk to the baby and show the baby how to roll the ball toward the pins. The older children get more practice counting the pins knocked down by a baby.

Toddlers will be eager to play. Though they tend to throw the ball instead of roll it, you may need to ask the older children to "teach" the toddler how to play. Let the older children count the pins knocked down by the toddler. The younger children learn to trust the older children and may seek their help in other situations.

∎

Matching

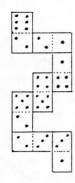

Matching things gets children actively involved in observing and exploring similarities and differences. Such distinctions help children understand relationships based on size, shape, color, name, and reason to classify. Classifying objects is an important logical skill.

Playing Animal Dominoes is a good beginning step towards helping young children match and sort. For toddlers and young 2 year olds: let them dump the animal cards or wooden animal dominoes out. Ask them to find a chick, a butterfly, a ladybug, bunny, cat as you arrange them into separate groupings. As they find the animals you ask for, help them match and place their domino with its group.

For the older children who want to play divide the dominoes among them. Explain the game by showing how one person places a domino on the floor or table, the next person matches that domino and the next person matches either domino at the end of the

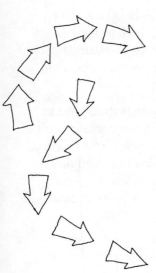

line. If game interest wanes, let them create their own designs and domino patterns (with or without matching). Children ready to count can play and count the pips (dots) on the dominoes.

Another good game that actively involves the mind and body is called Follow the Arrows. It can be modified to suit any developmental age.

Cut out a lot of paper arrows.

Make different paths of arrows all over the floor.

Draw different shapes on several pieces of paper and give each child a different shape.

At the end of each path leave pictures of the different shapes.

The children have to follow the arrows on the paths to find the shape that matches the one on their paper. Other variations include:

Place a pile of numbers at the end of each path. Hand each child a number card to find and match.

Give each child a color, and have them follow the path of arrows to match something at the end of the path with their color.

Place letters at the end of each path. Give each child different letters to find and match.

■

Classification Skills

Classification skills also include children's ability to subdivide things into different categories. For instance, Means of Transportation can be divided simply between cars and trucks for the very young.

Save cardboard tubes from paper towels or wrapping paper. Gather an assortment of small cars and trucks. Prop the tubes up on a slant and let the toddlers release the cars and trucks through the tubes down the "highway." They enjoy that element

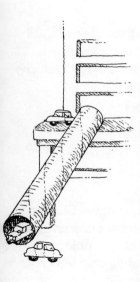

of surprise when the cars re-appear, and they see the relationship of cause and effect.

The older children will devise their own imaginary "highway" scene enjoying their cause and effect skills. They need little encouragement to build accompanying garages, repair shops, gas stations, apartment buildings, and hotels to complete the imaginary scene.

As the children develop thinking skills and language more categories can be realized, classified, and understood.

You can classify means of transportation even further:

> Unicycle: 1 wheel, 1 person, no handlebar
>
> Bicycle: 2 wheels, 1 person, handlebar
>
> Motorcycle: 2 wheels, 1 or 2 people, handlebar
>
> Tricycle: 3 wheels, 1 person, handlebar
>
> Helicopter: 0 wheels, 1–8 people, propeller
>
> Scooters: 4 wheels, 1 person, handlebar, body steers
>
> Skateboard: 8 wheels, 1 person, no handlebar, body steers
>
> Cars and Jeeps: 4 wheels, number of people depends on size of vehicle and number of seats, steering wheel
>
> Vans and Trucks: 4 wheels, number of people depends on size of vehicle and number of seats, steering wheel
>
> Trailers: 4 wheels, hitch onto 18 wheelers

Another way to develop classification skills creatively is to draw the same abstract shape onto each child's piece of paper. Let them draw anything and extend the shape into whatever they think it could be. What could a squiggle line become? How about a large inverted V shape? A sideways printed letter U? A square? You'll be surprised at what the children will create. From a simple picture to a complex scene the children will use their imaginations and classification skills to subdivide and even link things into various categories.

■

Divergent Thinking

Children are very creative and imaginative. Showing the same object to a group of different children can result in myriad ways to classify that one object. A game we play using this concept of flexible, divergent thinking involves giving each child a lump of Play-Doh®.

The instructions for this game are for the children to listen to a word and then mold their lump of Play-Doh® into a concept about that word. The results are amazing!

The first time we played, the group included 2 1/2 year old Matthew, 3 year olds Amanda, Jenny, and Kate, and 6 year olds Joseph and Eddie. I explained the instructions: that I would say a word and they try to make their Play-Doh® into anything they could think of relating to that word.

Initially I said the words, "washing machine." They immediately went to work. When everyone was done I asked each one to explain their work/concept. Matt had flattened out his lump of Play-Doh®, pressed his finger into the center to make a hole and announced, very matter-of-factly, "That's where you put the clothes in." Amanda had rolled her Play-Doh® into a long pencil shape, cut off a couple of pieces from the ends and pressed them into the rolled shape. She explained, "These are the clothes (the pieces she had cut off) hanging on this clothesline." (the long rolled shape). Jenny flattened down her lump of dough and poked three holes down the center. Jenny then said, "This is a shirt with three

buttons that needs to be washed." Kate squeezed the whole lump together and called it, "All the clothes to be washed!" Joseph cut away at his Play-Doh® to form the outline of pants and a shirt. Eddie's lump was cut out to form a shirt with·buttons and a pocket.

The next time we played, Joseph and Eddie were in school. The group consisted of Matthew, Jenny, Kate and two more 3 year olds, Robert and Candace. The word this time was "school." (Kate reminded me that Joseph and Eddie had played the game with them and were now in school.) Matt's round lump of Play-Doh® transformed into a representation of his older brother Jeff going off to school; Jenny's crude shape became a schoolbook; Kate's two round pieces with twig-shaped arms and legs symbolized "the teacher"; Robert flattened his Play-Doh® out as long as he possibly could and labeled it a ruler; Candace designed the school entrance door.

All of the children used flexible, divergent thinking to recognize, identify, sort, and classify images and shapes on the basis of their understanding logical classifications. Part of our job is to let them express those images creatively. Let them know it's all right to have different answers and ideas, and that these differences need to be expressed and accepted.

■

Shapes, Space, and Problem Solving

Puzzles help children begin to think and learn about solving problems. Have you noticed how even infants are problem solvers? The ability to imitate and store mental images of sights and sounds is necessary for the development of language and problem solving.

We have all heard the expression, "Out of sight, out of mind." You have probably also heard that for infants about six or seven months old this expression is literally true. If a toy the infant has just been playing with is blocked from view, the child will make no indication that the toy may stilll exist. But between eight and twelve months of age infants learn to solve problems. Create situations for babies to search for objects outside of their immediate field of vision.

For example let the baby see you hide a toy under your shirt, behind you, or under a blanket. See if the baby reaches and searches for it. (If too difficult yet, let a little part show.) Hide the toy behind the baby and in other places the baby can sit and/or reach.

Children often solve problems during the course of the day. We can learn to respect, acknowledge, and appreciate children's cognitive development when we observe them thinking. For instance, Brianne, 7 months old, and able to sit up but not yet mobile, spied a pile of library books just out of reach. Her favorite chunky board book was on top of this pile. I watched her pull the largest book at the bottom of the stack closer and closer until she could reach her own book on top. That was a difficult problem to solve. But she did it! And she could have had her pick of any book in that pile but she knew which one she wanted.

An excellent way to help babies solve a difficult dilemma is to set one up for them to figure out. Play these two games with them:

1. You will need two cups or containers, and a small toy or object. Hide the toy under one cup. Can the child find it?

2. Place a small object in the palm of your hand. Show the child both fists. Can the child select the fist with the small object in it? Continue playing alternating fists. This is a game of anticipation and memory with that element of surprise and discovery!

Nesting cups or a set of measuring cups are good tools for children to experiment with to try to fit objects of different sizes together. Nesting cups require the visual discrimination skill of comparing small vs. large.

Do you remember the game where someone hides a pebble or marble in their fist, you have to guess which fist has the pebble or marble in it, and if you pick the right fist you move up one step? This wonderful game of good guessing could be adapted for any age to enjoy.

As children develop, their thinking develops. The games they are developmentally able to understand and toys they find interesting to play with coincide with new thinking skills. Observing children as their thinking develops is delightful. I asked 18 month old Tyler to come and put his coat on to go outside. He ran to me. He had a bristle block in one hand. As I held the jacket for him to put his arm in the sleeve, he knew to transfer the block to the other hand! That may seem so simplistic to us but it is a thinking process. He was able to transfer information from the left side of his brain to the right side. What if it had been a cookie he was holding and he hadn't changed hands?

Tinkertoys®, shape sorters, blocks, tool kits, puzzles, and large and small pegs and pegboards are subtle educational toys that increase a young child's ability to fit things together, see relationships, and take them apart both cognitively and physically. Social behavior, language development, and math concepts will emerge from the toys children have to work

Chapter 17

An Introduction to Early Childhood Geometry

■

Understanding Basic Shapes

Children learn by doing. They have to see shapes, hear you describe the shapes, and find them on their own in order to understand that math can be fun!

Start by tracing the rim of the children's juice cups and by talking about circles. Next, point to and trace the outer edge of a plate, the cap of a juice bottle, the base of the bottle, a bowl; show the children any common object with a circular shape. Once you get started looking around the room, calling out objects, and showing the children different items with circular shapes, they quickly join in. They search and scrounge around observing everything trying to select and determine where the circles are. Magnets, buttons, eyeballs, oven dials, door knobs, oranges, the letter "o" (lower case, of course), polka dots, the holes of a strainer, nostrils, and cantaloupes are only some of the circles the children have just discovered. And we haven't even left the kitchen! In the case of oranges and cantaloupes, tasting the circular shape would help reinforce active learning. The pattern hasn't changed, they are still learning through their senses. Later in the day begin this game in a different room or when you go outdoors.

On another day try squares, then rectangles, triangles, and ovals. You will be surprised how many shapes the children can actually uncover. You are giving them yet another avenue to become more aware of their environment through their refined sensorimotor skills. They begin to look at things differently, critically. You give them opportunities to understand a basic shape and realize its possibilities. A rectangle, for instance, has the potential of being a picture frame, a TV screen, a brick, a door, an entire area rug, an entire room! Just as the potential to recognize objects as shapes grows, so too does potential active learning.

■

A Homemade Shape Game

Put items in the shape of circles, squares, rectangles, triangles, and ovals into a shoe box or pillowcase. Suggestions for shapes to use might include:

> **Circles:** bottle caps, blocks, buttons, jar lids, saucers
>
> **Squares:** pot holders, Tupperware® containers, blocks
>
> **Rectangles:** index cards, envelopes, blocks
>
> **Triangles:** magnets, Hershey's® kiss, blocks
>
> **Ovals:** grapes, beads, eggs

Let the children reach in the box, select one item, and figure out its shape. Talk about their sizes: big, bigger, biggest; large, larger, largest; long, longer, longest. Young children increase their cognitive development and their language skills by listening, playing, and identifying the objects in the box.

■

A Play-Doh® Shape Puzzle

❏ **IF** you have a rolling pin and Play-Doh®, and a group of 2, 3, 4 and 5 year olds;

❏ **THEN** you can create a Play-Doh® shape puzzle.

❏ **HOW?** Let the children roll out their Play-Doh®

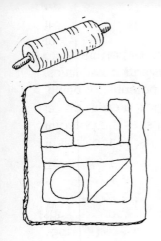

Cut out small and large different shapes from each child's flattened Play-Doh® and remove these shapes.

Place the cut out shapes in front of each child and ask them to fit the cut out shapes back into their rolled out Play-Doh®.

Talk about and find the small circles, big squares, the largest triangle, the longest oval.

■

Baking = Holistic Math

❏ **IF** you bake with the children in your care;

❏ **THEN** you can also make a Shape Puzzle out of cookie dough to bake and eat!

❏ **HOW?** To make rolled sugar cookies:

Preheat oven to 400°.

3/4 cup of soft margarine or butter

3/4 cup sugar

2 eggs

1/2 teaspoon vanilla

2 1/2 cups sifted all-purpose flour

1 teaspoon baking powder

1/2 teaspoon salt

Beat butter until creamy. Beat in sugar and eggs. Add vanilla. Then, beat flour into mixture to form a stiff, smooth dough. Chill at least 1 hour.

Break off small pieces of dough for each child to roll out. Let the children form their own shapes, cut into shapes, or use cookie cutters. Place on ungreased cookie sheet. Bake for 6 minutes, remove from oven, and cool. Have the children identify the shapes before they eat them.

❏ **WHY?** Baking is an experience children enjoy with or without shapes. But safety first—always! Talk about the dangers of knives, hot ovens, hot cookie sheets and baking pans.

Cooking and baking is active learning. Children learn that printed words offer valuable information. Read the directions aloud to the children. Read the recipe to the children. Think of the new words you can introduce. Think of the concepts cooking and baking touch upon.

The *mathematical concepts* include: counting eggs, comparing teaspoons and tablespoons, comparing 1/2 cup to 1 cup—show the children the difference with flour, sugar, milk, or water, measuring ingredients with measuring spoons and measuring cups, counting cookies, muffins, or popcorn.

The *science concepts* include: how heat can change things, how adding different ingredients changes liquids and solids, or how yeast causes bread to rise.

The *artistic concepts* include: decorating a cake, decorating cookies with glaze, creating designs with raisins, chopped nuts, chocolate chips, or sprinkles.

The *social concepts* include: working together in a group, taking turns (with rolling pin or stirring), comparing and measuring, learning with friends, sharing ideas, sharing the experience with parents, sharing the baked goods with friends and parents.

■

Baked Clay Shapes

Mix together: 4 cups flour, 2 cups water, and 1 cup salt.

Let the children roll pieces of clay dough into whatever shapes they like. Place their shapes on wax paper to dry overnight. Heat oven to 300°.

Bake for one hour on ungreased cookie sheet. Let the children paint their shapes when cool. When the paint dries let the children apply clear varnish to each shape to protect them from chipping.

Initiating New Math Ideas

There are times when I am ready to initiate or introduce a new game or an idea, but while observing the children at play I realize my timing would be an intrusion. Your ideas have to be extensions of child's play to be accepted and understood by them. Children need to be alert, curious, and confident in their ability to think things out for themselves. Jerome Bruner (as cited in Lawrence,1978) claims, "the knowledge that makes sense to a learner is likely to lead to further learning."

Blending your thoughts and actions into the thinking and playing of children leads to further learning. I respect the children and their ideas and believe their learning stems from activities that are self-initiated, self-directed, and caregiver supported. For example, one afternoon four of the children were involved working on different puzzles. Two 5 year olds worked jointly on a sixty-three piece puzzle and a 4 -1/2 year old was helping a 2 year old put together an eight piece wooden puzzle. I waited for them to finish and then asked if they wanted to figure out a different type of puzzle; I wanted to introduce Chinese tangrams.

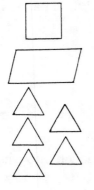

Tangram is a Chinese puzzle popularized throughout Asia, Europe, and the U.S. during the 1840s. "According to encyclopedic lore, the game of Tangram is of very ancient origin, and has been played in China for upward of 4,000 years. . ." (S. Loyd, 1968). A Tangram involves fitting a square, a parallelogram, and five triangles together to form various patterns. You can make your own Tangram puzzle out of cardboard or felt material.

Each child selected a pattern they would attempt to copy from *The Eighth Book of Tan* by Sam Loyd (1968). Five year old Joseph picked the puzzle of a baby carriage; 5 year old Lauren selected a swan; 4 1/2 year old Jeffrey tried to re-create the flower; and 2 year old Kate wanted to copy the puzzle of a man. What appears so simplistic is truly a puzzle. After many attempts I assured each child that their original Tangram creations were just as fun to look at and figure out as the puzzles in the book. I wanted to avoid any frustration of not being able to copy the puzzles in the book.

Tangram puzzles offer children a chance to play with shapes while actively practicing and using logical thinking skills. The original designs offered creative, aesthetic work and play—what Jerome Bruner

Chapter 18

Making Sense of Numbers

■

Helping Children Understand the Purpose of Numbers

For children to gain a better understanding of numbers and their different meanings they need developmentally appropriate opportunities that suit their interests and physical abilities. Children need many activities and plenty of time to play and to build conceptual bridges and learn from their experiences.

Activities that let children actively match, measure, observe, compare, and count are necessary preliminary experiences young children need to understand the meaning of numbers. A lot of children know how to count; however, they don't realize that each number they are reciting means a specific amount; or represents a one-to-one correspondence—pairing objects together such as: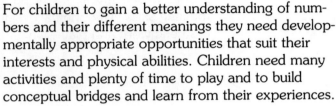

or the concept of conservation—where the number of objects remains the same but their arrangement may change. To a young child six apples spread out on a table may look like more than six apples piled up in a bowl. Or, consider this grouping.

■ ■ ■ ■

■　■　■　■

To a preschooler there appears to be more big squares due to their arrangement and size.

■
One-to-One Correspondence

Playing dominoes encourages children to see a one-to-one correspondence because the dominoes have to match. Fitting pegs in a pegboard and playing with marbles on a Chinese checker board are other ways to help children arrange objects in one-to-one correspondence. Here is another ingenious one-to-one correspondence activity called Lunch For Sale.

One afternoon I put penny price tags on all of the childrens' lunch items. I tagged their plates, napkins, cups, even their sandwiches with price tags taped to toothpicks!

I gave them pennies to put in their pockets. They pretended to come to my luncheonette to "buy" each item needed for lunch. They carefully counted out their pennies to purchase each item. It was certainly a novel activity. They were quite surprised and eager to cooperate. I knew that this learning experience was a success because they continued "buying and selling" napkins, cups, forks, and spoons even after lunch! Most of their pleasure came from playing with real napkins, their real juice cups, and especially real money. This playful experience made learning one-to-one correspondence fun.

■
The Toy Store Computer Check-Out

Most toys and stuffed animals have a manufacturer's number or serial number on them somewhere. To play Toy Store, the children come to the checkout counter (me) and show me the toy or animal they want to buy. I type the name of their item into the computer while they are busy locating that manufacturer's number (the pretend price of the item). Once found, they type in this purchase price and pretend they are buying gifts.

You don't even need a computer; a piece of paper or a typewriter serves the same purpose. Even a hand-held calculator lets the children input the numbers from their "purchases."

If the children like, have them "dress-up" to come shopping: in long dresses, or as race car drivers, police officers, firefighters, bakers, astronauts, or an emergency medical team. This adds a new, major dimension! The children choose what they need to buy depending on who they are pretending to be.

■

Measuring

I had a footstool with a loose leg (which I had purposely loosened). I gave each child a ruler and asked them to measure the "broken" leg of the footstool for me. I explained that with their help measuring I would know the right size needed to replace the broken leg.

Even though I got a different measurement from each child, they were eager to assist. I asked them to see if any of the other legs were loose. They checked and measured each one. Then they proceeded to measure the couch legs, every chair leg, table legs, the rise of each stair and the length of my rug—by putting all of their rulers together. I was not looking for or expecting accuracy. I was providing another means for the children to understand the mathematical concept of associating numbers and measuring. Even the accuracy will develop through play.

Card Games

Card games are useful to encourage mathematical concepts in 3, 4, and 5 year olds. Through card games children can practice:

1. recognizing certain numbers,

2. making sets of two, three, or four that are alike (by suit) or identical (by number),

3. arranging cards in order or in a series,

4. judging which card has "more than" or "less than,"

5. matching cards either by number or suit,

6. making sets of three or four-of-a-kind.

An Innovative Math Lesson

Given a deck of cards and a homemade spinner wheel (a paper plate with sections numbered from 1 to 10 and a cardboard arrow tacked on) the children devised their own lesson in recognizing numbers. Their game included number recognition, matching, choosing, taking turns being spinner and number caller, cooperation, and participation. To play, each child was given a set of cards in a series from Ace (one) to ten. I usually omit jacks, queens, and kings from card games when playing with young children. Another important value to recognize and acknowledge is each child agreeing on taking turns being the spinner/number caller. Joseph, 4 years old, was first. Lauren and Jessica, 4 1/2 years old, and Jeffrey, 4, each selected and held up one card from their 1–10 series of cards and told Joseph which number they had selected. Joseph would spin the wheel as each anticipated the fate of the arrow. If the arrow chose the number they selected that person became the spinner/caller.

As a by-product of their game Jessica introduced her friends to saying the words in French. Jessica speaks French in her home and they played their number spin game trying to call the numbers out in French with Jessica's help.

This innovative math lesson thus served a dual purpose: the children learned to name the numbers—both in English and French—and they showed an active interest in and appreciation of another child's culture.

■
■
■
■

PART SIX

Conclusion and Bibliography

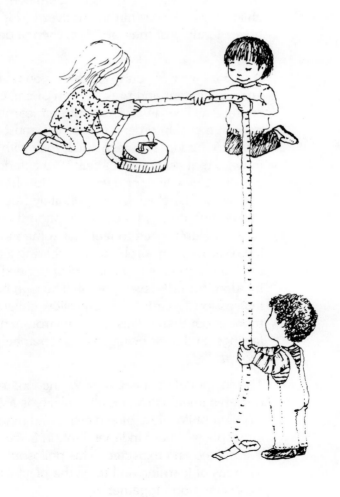

Conclusion

Enjoy yourself and the children! The encouragement children receive from you in their work and play and in their thinking develops considerable self-confidence and independence. To help children develop accompanying self-regulation skills that maintain their motivation to learn is to give them the opportunity to know and appreciate themselves. In doing so they learn to feel appreciated. Children need you to recognize their efforts, reassure their abilities, and affirm their actions to learn to feel good about themselves. This foundation of confidence you help children develop within themselves builds that deeper understanding of their abilities when undertaking any task.

As a caregiver of young children, you need to offer encouragement and preservation of children's creative abilities in all areas of their learning and development. In order to do so you must remain open to the ideas of each child. Play with their ideas in ways that accept and attempt to extend and construct new and/or diverse relationships and concepts. The children are definitely free to respond and contribute any bit of information they have to offer. Children need to feel that someone is listening. Questioning, probing, and sharing ideas builds trust and a mutual respect. Children need to have freedom for self-development. Through brainstorming sessions your interactions allow children to learn more about themselves, their environment, their feelings, and their being valuable members of a group.

The methodology necessary to encourage and preserve imaginative, creative ability is actually my working philosophy of achieving and maintaining an atmosphere where independent, individual discovery is accepted and expected. This philosophy applies to all areas of learning and to all the playful activities we decide upon together.

Introducing young children to shared experiences and activities occupies the middle ground between the two opposing theories of education Robert Havighurst (1952) describes in *Developmental Tasks and Education*. Havighurst's developmental task concept lies between the theory of freedom—that children will develop if left as free as possible; and the theory of constraint—that children will learn to become worthy responsible adults through positive approvals and behavioral restraints imposed by the decent values of caregivers and society.

Rules and expectations that are encountered daily hopefully set self-regulatory processes in motion in the minds of young children when interacting within a group. Playing games with 3, 4, and 5 year olds can be a healthy and satisfactory involvement provided the children are free to create and practice their newly acquired physical and intellectual skills. When I introduce a game I explain the prescribed set of rules as a reference; however, such rules are rarely enforced. By understanding their intellectual level, their physical ability, and the degree of interest each child has produces creative, flexible, opportunities. Children do want and certainly need boundaries to understand and know acceptable behavior. They don't want to be out of control. Help them exercise control when it is needed. Self-regulatory skills are important toward developing autonomy and the ability to interact and function as a valuable member of a group. This underlying principle creates a cohesive yet individual, empathetic, active, and able group of children. Maintaining this philosophy is a developmental task requiring intelligence and understanding, imagination and flexibility—not an application of formulas.

Achieving an appropriate dependent-independent atmosphere stems from techniques expressed by Maslow, Rogers, Kelley, and Combs in *Perceiving, Behaving, Becoming* (1962), who said "that each person is worthy of respect; that each person grows continuously from birth to death merging the past into the now; that each is a product of an inner core developed and modified by experience; that interaction with people is the strongest environmental determinant in the self-concept; that when the environment is basically unthreatening, the individual's own behavior toward elements in the environment is open, self-and-others trusting, interactive, sympathetic and constructive, and that in such an environment dignity, integrity and autonomy emerge as characteristics of people."* Creating such an atmosphere is the most appropriate method to encourage a child's creative possibilities.

---

* Maslow, A., C. R. Rogers, H. Kelley, and A. Combs, *Perceiving, Behaving, Becoming* (Washington, D.C.: Association for Supervision and Curriculum Development, National Education Association, 1962).

Bibliography

Ainsworth, Mary, D. Salter, M. C. Blehar, E. Waters, and S. Wall. *Patterns of Attachment: Assessed in the Strange Situation and at Home.* Hillside, N.J.: Erlbaum, 1978.

Applebee, Arthur N., and Judith A. Langer. "Instructional Scaffolding: Reading and Writing as Natural Language Activities." *Language Arts* 60, no. 2 (1983): 168–175.

Ardley, Neil. *Music: An Illustrated Encyclopedia.* New York and Oxford: Facts on File Publishers, 1986.

Brandt, Ronald. "Discipline Based Art Education: An Interview with Elliot Eisner." *Educational Leadership* 45 (December 1987/January 1988): 6–9.

Brandt, Ronald. "On Assessment in the Arts: A Conversation with Howard Gardner." *Educational Leadership* 45 (December 1987/ January 1988): 30–34.

Brazelton, T. Berry. *Infants and Mothers, Differences in Development.* New York: Delacorte Press/Seymour Lawrence, 1969.

Brazelton, T. Berry. *Toddlers and Parents, A Declaration of Independence.* New York: Delacorte Press/Seymour Lawrence, 1974.

Bruner, Jerome S. *The Process of Education.* Cambridge, Mass.: Harvard University Press, 1960.

Bruner, Jerome S. *Toward a Theory of Instruction.* Cambridge, Mass.: The Belknap Press of Harvard University Press, 1966.

Caduto, Michael J. and Joseph Bruchac, *Keepers of the Earth.* Golden, Colorado: Fulcrum, Inc., 1989.

Cartwright, Sally. "Play Can Be the Blocks of Learning." *Young Children* (July 1988): 44–47.

Cataldo, Christine Z. *Infant and Toddler Programs.* Reading, Mass.: Addison-Wesley Publishing Co., 1983.

Cazden, Courtney, ed. *Language in Early Childhood Education.* Washington, D.C.: National Association for the Education of Young Children, 1981.

Chinaberry Book Service. *Books and Music for Children and Families.* Spring Valley, Ca.: Chinaberry Book Service, 1991.

Cullinan, Bernice E., and Carolyn W. Carmichael, eds. *Literature and Young Children.* Urbana, Ill.: National Council of Teachers of English, 1977.

D'Amico, Victor. *Creative Teaching in Art.* Scranton, Pa.: International Textbook Co., 1953.

Dennis, W., and Y. Sayegh. "The Effect of Supplementary Experiences Upon the Behavioral Development of Infants in Institutions." *Child Development* 36 (1965): 81–90.

Dobbert, Marion Lundy. "Play Is Not Monkey Business: A Holistic Biocultural Perspective on the Role of Play in Learning." *Educational Horizons* (Summer 1985): 161.

Durrell, Gerald. *Amateur Naturalist.* New York: Alfred A. Knopf Publishing Co., 1988.

E.L.F. *Early Learning Fun.* Aurora, Ill.: Project ELF Task Force, 1976.

Edwards, Betty. *Drawing on the Right Side of the Brain.* Los Angeles, Ca.: J. P. Tarcher, Inc., 1979.

Eisner, Elliot W. *Readings in Art Education.* Waltham, Mass.: Blaisdell Publishing Co., a division of Ginn and Co., 1966.

Eliason, Claudia Fuhrman, and Loa Thomas Jenkins. *A Practical Guide to Early Child Education.* St. Louis, Mo.: The C. V. Mosby Co., 1977.

Elkind, David. *Miseducation Preschoolers at Risk.* New York: Alfred A. Knopf, 1987.

Erikson, Erik. *Childhood and Society.* New York: W. W. Norton and Co., 1963.

Filstrup, Jane Merrill. *Monday Through Friday, Day Care Alternatives.* New York: Teachers College Press, Columbia University, 1982.

Fleming, Bonnie, and Diane Hamilton. *Resource for Creative Teaching in Early Childhood Education.* New York: Harcourt Brace Jovanovich, 1979.

Fraiberg, Selma. *The Magic Years.* New York: Charles Scribner's Sons, 1959.

Gardner, Howard. *Artful Scribbles: The Significance of Children's Drawings.* New York: Basic Books, 1980.

Grant, Carl. *In Praise of Diversity: A Resource Book for Multicultural Education.* Washington, D.C.: Association of Teacher Education, 1977.

Hartley, Ruth E., Lawrence K. Frank, and Robert M. Goldenson. *Understanding Children's Play.* New York: Columbia University Press, 1952.

Havighurst, Robert J. *Developmental Tasks and Education.* New York: David McKay and Co., 1952.

Healy, Jane M. *Your Child's Growing Mind.* Garden City, N.Y.: Doubleday and Co., 1987.

Helms, Donald B., and Jeffrey S. Turner. *Exploring Child Behavior.* Philadelphia, Pa.: W. B. Saunders Co., 1976.

Hirsch, Elizabeth. *The Block Book.* Washington, D.C.: National

Association for the Education of Young Children, 1984.

Hohmann, Mary, Bernard Bonet, and David Weikart. *Young Children in Action: A Manual for Preschool Education*. Ypsilanti, Mi.: High Scope Education Press, 1979.

Kamii, Constance, and Rheta DeVries. *Group Games in Early Education*. Washington, D.C.: National Association for the Education of Young Children, 1980.

Keen, Martin L. *The How and Why Wonder Book of Science Experiments*. Los Angeles, Ca.: Price/Stern/Sloan Publishers, 1985.

Kelly, Marguerite, and Elia Parsons. *The Mother's Almanac*. New York: Doubleday, 1975.

Lansing, Kenneth M. "Art and the Child: Are They Compatible?" *Studies in Art Education* 28 (Fall 1986): 11–15.

Larche, Douglas. *Father Gander Nursery Rhymes*. Santa Barbara, Ca.: Advocacy Press, 1985.

Lawrence, Gordon D. "Bruner's Instructional Theory or Curriculum Theory?" *Theory into Practice* Vol. 8 (18–24).

Lowenfeld, Viktor. *Your Child and His Art*. New York: Macmillan Co., 1954.

Loyd, Sam. *The Eighth Book of Tan*. New York: Dover Publishing Co., 1968.

Maeroff, Gene I. *The School-Smart Parent*. New York: Time Books, a division of Random House, 1989.

Mahler, Margaret. *The Psychological Birth of the Human Infant*. New York: Basic Books, 1975.

Marzollo, Jean, and Janice Lloyd. *Learning Through Play*. New York: Harper and Row, 1972.

Maslow, A., C. R. Rogers, H. Kelley, and A. Combs. *Perceiving, Behaving, Becoming*. Washington, D.C.: Association for Supervision and Curriculum Development, National Education Association, 1962.

McKim, Robert H. *Thinking Visually, A Strategy Manual for Problem Solving*. Belmont, Ca.: Lifetime Learning Publications, a division of Wadsworth, 1980.

McPherson, Mark. *Choosing Your Pet*. Mahwan, N.J.: Troll Associates, 1985.

Moché, Dinah. *Magic Science Tricks*. New York: Scholastic, Inc., 1977.

Piaget, Jean. *The Language and Thought of the Child*. Cleveland, Ohio: World Publishing Co., 1955.

Piaget, Jean. *The Origins of Intelligence in Children*. New York: New York International University Press, 1974.

Read, Katherine H. *The Nursery School.* Philadelphia, Pa.: W. B. Saunders Co., 1971.

Reader's Digest *ABC's of Nature, A Family Answer Book.* Pleasantville, N.Y.: Reader's Digest Association, November 1985.

Reader's Digest Edition, *Birds: Their Life • Their Ways • Their World.* Pleasantville, N.Y.: Reader's Digest Association, 1979.

Reeves, Martha Emilie. *The Total Turtle.* New York: Thomas Y. Crowell Co., 1975.

Rheingold, H. L., and C. O. Eckerman. "The Infant Separates Himself from His Mother." *Science* 168 (1970): 78-83.

Rinard, Judith E. *Helping Our Animal Friends, Books for Young Explorers.* Washington, D.C.: National Geographic Society, 1985.

Rossi, Mary Jane Mangini. *Read to Me! Teach Me!* Wauwatosa, Wi.: American Baby Books, 1982.

Roy, Ron. *What Has Ten Legs and Eats Corn Flakes?* New York: Clarion Books, Tichnor and Fields, a Houghton Mifflin Co., 1982.

Schell, Robert E., and Elizabeth Hall. *Developmental Psychology Today.* New York: Random House, 1979.

Silverstein, Alvin and Virginia. *World of the Brain.* New York: William Morrow and Co., Inc., 1986.

Spodek, Bernard. *Teaching in the Early Years.* Englewood Cliffs, N.J.: Prentice-Hall, 1972.

Springer, Sally, and Georg Deutsch. *Left Brain, Right Brain.* San Francisco, Ca.: W. H. Freeman and Co., 1981.

Stewart, Doug. "Teachers Aim at Turning Loose the Mind's Eye." *Smithsonian* (August 1985): 44–56.

Taylor, Barbara J. *A Child Goes Forth.* Provo, Utah: Brigham Young University Press, 1975.

Thomson, David S. *language.* New York: Time-Life Books, 1975.

Voris, Helen H., Maija Sedzielarz, and Carolyn P. Blackmon. *Teach the Mind, Touch The Spirit.* Chicago, Ill.: Department of Education, Field Museum of Natural History, 1986.

Wessells, Katherine Tyler. *The Golden Songbook.* New York: Golden Press, a division of Western Publishing Co., Racine, Wi., 1981.

White, Burton L. "An Experimental Approach to the Effects of Experience on Early Human Behavior." In *Minnesota Symposia on Child Psychology,* vol. 1, J. P. Hill, ed., 201–226. Minneapolis: University of Minnesota Press, 1967.

Yawkey, Thomas D., and Anthony D. Pellegrini. *Child's Play: Developmental and Applied.* Hillside, N.J.: Erlbaum, 1984.

Sources for Further Reading

■

One helpful way to feel comfortable in the world of children is to write for publications that provide insight, information, and a necessary sense of emotional support. The National Association of Family Day Care (NAFDC) provides publications to encourage and educate providers. Write to NAFDC at 725 15th Street, NW, #505, Washington, D.C. 20005, or call 1–202–347–3356.

Better Baby Care: A Book for Family Day Care Providers (NAFDC)

Child Care in a Family Setting, A Comprehensive Guide to Family Day Care by Vijay T. Jaisinghani and Vivian Gunn Morris (1985). Philadelphia, Pa., Family Care Associates and Community College.

Day-Care Providers Easy Bookkeeping System (NAFDC)

Explore and Create: Activities for Young Children (NAFDC)

Family Day Care and You (1989). A basic curriculum for the challenging and important career of home child care. Rhode Island College Department of Social and Rehabilitative Services Home Day Care Training Program.

Family Day Caring (1989). Toys 'n Things Press, 450 North Syndicate Suite 5, St. Paul, Minnesota 55104.

Finger Frolics: Fingerplays for Young Children (NAFDC)

Handbook for Home Care of Children (1984). Wayne State University, Child Development Training Program, 166 Old Main, Wayne State University, Detroit, Michigan 48202.

Iowa Family Day Care Handbook (1979). Information and Ideas Resources. Iowa State University Child Development Training Program, Department of Child Development. (There is a $3.00 charge made payable to Iowa State University.)

NAFDC Accreditation Program Study Guide (NAFDC)

A Practical Guide for Day Care Personnel by John L. DeLorey and Marjorie E. Cahn. (1977). Day Care and Child Development Council of America, Inc., 622 14th Street, NW, Washington, D.C. 20005.

The Provider Connection (NAFDC)

"Starting Your Own Family Day Care Business" (NAFDC)

Spoonful of Lovin': A Manual For Day Care Providers by Annette Lubchenco (1981). Mile High Child Care Association, Agency for Instructional Television, Box A, Bloomington, Indiana 48402.

The Winning Family: Increasing Self-Esteem in Your Children and Yourself by Dr. Louise Hart. (NAFDC)

■

Periodical Subscriptions

Subscribing to newsletters, periodicals, or magazines provides a steady source of ideas and support for parents and providers to stay abreast of the knowledge on current child development findings, studies, and trends. A few good periodicals include:

Argus: The Journal of Family Day Care
P.O. Box 15146
Atlanta, Georgia 30333

Beginnings
Box 2890
Redmond, Washington 98073

Child Care Information Exchange
Box 2890
Redmond, Washington 98073

Child Care Quarterly
Human Services Press
72 Fifth Avenue
New York, New York 10011

Day Care and Early Education
Human Sciences Press
72 Fifth Avenue
New York, New York 10011

Family Day Caring
Toys 'n Things Press
A Division of Resources for Child Caring
450 North Syndicate Suite 5
St. Paul, Minnesota 55104

Young Children
National Association for the Education of Young Children
1834 Connecticut Avenue, NW
Washington, D.C. 20001
(Subscription range from $12.00 to $30.00 a year.)

Sources for Reference and Business Aspects of Child Care

Local state agencies can provide resources and reference material necessary for you to register, certify, encourage, and build your family day care home business. Before you get started it is best to check with your state agency to comply with ordinances and zoning variances. Here is a sampling of organizations that provide newsletters, publications, conferences, and general helpful information:

Association for Children of New Jersey
17 Academy Street, Suite 709
Newark, New Jersey 07102
1–201–643–3876

Child Care Law Center
625 Market Street, Suite 816
San Francisco, California 94105
1–415–495–5408

The Children's Foundation
122 "C" Street, NW
Washington, D.C. 20001
1–202–628–8787

Clearinghouse on Elementary and Early Childhood Education ERIC/EECE
College of Education
University of Illinois
805 W. Pennsylvania Avenue
Urbana, Illinois 61801
1–217–333–1386

National Association for the Education of Young Children (NAEYC)
1834 Connecticut Avenue, NW
Washington, D.C. 20009
1–800–424–2460 or 1–202–232–8777

Save the Children/Child Care Support Center
1182 W. Peachtree Street, NW
Atlanta, Georgia 30309
1–404–885–1578

Index